BOXING

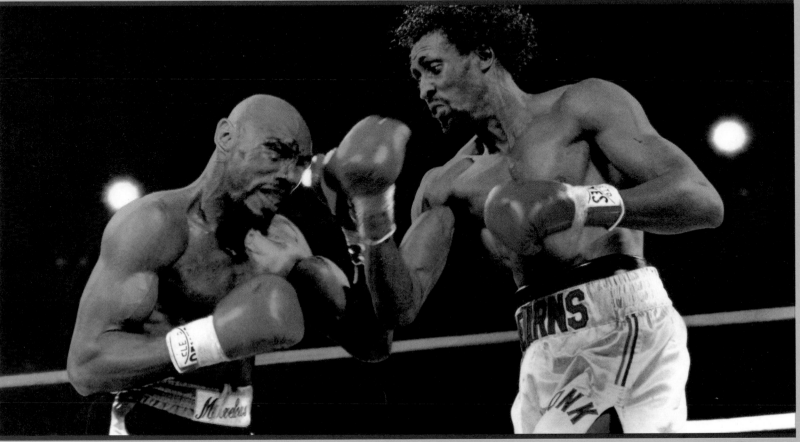

LEGENDS

Greatest Boxers... Toughest Fights... Classic Rivalries

Angus G. Garber III

GALLERY BOOKS
An Imprint of W. H. Smith Publishers Inc.
112 Madison Avenue
New York, New York 10016

A FRIEDMAN GROUP BOOK

Published by GALLERY BOOKS
An imprint of W.H. Smith Publishers, Inc.
112 Madison Avenue
New York, New York 10016

ISBN 0-8317-0999-5

*BOXING LEGENDS: The Greatest Boxers, Toughest Fights, and
Classic Rivalries*
was prepared and produced by
Michael Friedman Publishing Group, Inc.
15 West 26th Street
New York, New York 10010

Editor: Sharon Kalman
Art Director/Designer: Mary Moriarty
Photo Editor: Christopher Bain
Photo Researcher: Daniella Nilva
Production Manager: Karen L. Greenberg

Typeset by I, CLAVDIA Inc.
Color separations by South Sea International Press Ltd.
Printed and bound in Hong Kong by Leefung-Asco Printers Ltd.

DEDICATION

For Gerry, who still understands

ACKNOWLEDGMENTS

Many thanks to the fighters who shared their time and memories;
the experts at The Ring; my mother, the tenacious reference librarian;
Jim Shea, the marvelous writer for the *Hartford Courant;*
Michael Friedman Publishing Group editor Bruce Lubin;
and Tony Wicks of the *Morristown Record.*

CONTENTS

UPI/Bettmann NewsPhotos

INTRODUCTION

There is something viscerally compelling about a prizefight. It doesn't get more basic than this: Two men in a square ring with nothing more between them than light leather gloves and a will to win. Boxing was no doubt the original sport, and has survived to this day because it taps our deepest instincts for survival.

From the beginning of civilization man has fought, usually to protect his possessions. Now, a champion fights to protect his title, proving that boxing is still a matter of territorial imperative. Combatants no longer go at it bare-knuckled in a field or on a street corner. Like society, boxing has grown more sophisticated over the years.

On September 10, 1927, some 104,943 spectators jammed into Chicago's Soldier Field to watch Gene Tunney fight Jack Dempsey for the world heavyweight championship. The gate generated that day was $2,659,660, a record that stood until 1978. For the thirty-nine minutes Tunney needed to earn a second consecutive ten-round decision, he took home $990,445, a fair piece of change. Today, it is possible for a man like Marvelous Marvin Hagler—that's his legal name in this business where marketing means everything—to earn more than twelve million dollars in an hour's work, despite losing the decision as he did to Sugar Ray Leonard in 1987. And though crowds don't attend fights the way they used to, today's communications network can transform the world into a global village. Millions are linked to the gladiators' arena via closed circuit television.

There is a price extracted for these staggering glories. More often than not, it is a pound of the fighter's flesh—and mind. For hand-to-hand combat takes its toll on the body and the head, which both receive punches. That's why people acting dazed or bewildered are often called punch-drunk. The American Medical Association has called for the banning of boxing on the grounds that it exacts a cruel and unusual punishment on the human body. There is strong evidence to support the theory. Seven men have died while engaged in a world title fight, with welterweight Benny Paret of Cuba as the most notable fatality. When South Korea's Duk-Koo Kim died at the hands of lightweight Ray Mancini, the hue and cry began anew. But for every Duk-Koo Kim there are dozens of Willie Peps, who after 242 career bouts as a featherweight, is thriving today at the age of sixty-six in a Connecticut government job. "Hey," Pep reasons, "you've got to take risks in life to get ahead." In boxing the contrast between success and failure is just more clearly defined.

The object of boxing—separating a man from his senses—hasn't changed much from the days of Jersey Joe Walcott, below, to Sugar Ray Leonard. The purses, however, have increased dramatically.

Keystone/FPG Intl.

Randolph Turpin, right, stunned the boxing world in 1951 when he caught middleweight champion Sugar Ray Robinson with flurry after flurry of sharp blows. Turpin lifted the title in July but lost it two months later when Robinson stopped him in the tenth round.

THE
SWEET SCIENCE

Boxing, despite its rather elegant moniker, is not a science of sweetness and light. It was Pierce Egan, an early nineteenth century English sports writer who first used the term "The Sweet Science." In the 1950s, A.J. Liebling of *The New Yorker* popularized the term in a book of the same name, borrowed from Egan's collection of essays titled "Boxiana." Perhaps because of the money it generates, the unseemly promoters who run it, or the invariable environment of its purveyors—dimly lit gyms that smell of sweat and broken dreams—boxing is seen as a brutal business. But, in fact, the sport paints a colorful canvas stretched over a generally unseemly history. This is one of boxing's charms. Look at a George Bellows' painting. See the smokey haze rising above the ring. Hear the crowd. Smell the effort. Feel the heat. Bellows, an early 20th century social realist, whose paintings were imbued with a sense of life, may have captured boxing best.

Don King, the flamboyant promoter, is an example of all that boxing is. King once served time on a manslaughter charge in Cleveland, where he ran a numbers racket; he is now one of boxing's biggest power merchants. His hair stands on end as if it were shocked into attention; his mouth never stops—and neither do the proceeds of the fights he hypes. King wears gaudy jewelry and is equally comfortable quoting Shakespeare or Martin Luther King. He is a self-made man who, like Tex Rickard before him, understands the game. Rickard masterminded the Gene Tunney-Jack Dempsey fights that drew six-figure crowds and earned seven-figure gates.

Today, however, billboards and placards don't cut it. Big fights have become carefully orchestrated media events with catchy, official titles like "The Thrilla in Manila," or "The War at the Shore." Big fights follow a promotion formula. After much speculation and posturing by both sides, the fight is set. Fighter A says he's going to knock out Fighter B in the third round—if he's lucky. Fighter B says Fighter A's mother wears Army boots. And so on. If the promoter and the fighters have done their job (and the baying media hounds have taken the bone), enough people will fill the seats, at both the arena and closed circuit locations, to insure a profit. Often, the fight pales in comparison to the hype itself.

After the bout, the loser will invariably claim that he caught a thumb in his right eye. Or his cold medication slowed his punches. Or losing too much weight too quickly sapped his strength.

Or something.

The vast amounts of money involved have always induced great fighters to hang on long past their prime. This happens in all sports, but boxing's endings are particularly unhappy. Joe Louis, at the age of thirty-seven, was knocked out by future heavyweight champion Rocky Marciano. At thirty-eight, Muhammad Ali was knocked out by heavyweight champion Larry Holmes. In 1985, Holmes himself would lose his chance to equal Marcino's unmatched 49-0 record by losing to Michael Spinks; Holmes was just short of his thirty-sixth birthday. In 1987, Great Britain's Joe Bugner, thirty-seven, agreed to fight fellow countryman Frank Bruno, twenty-five. Bugner had not been in the ring for nearly five years, but the lure of thirty-five thousand spectators paying more than four million dollars to see a reincarnation of their former heavyweight hero was too much for Bugner and his promoters to pass up.

Boxing has always been synonymous with gambling, and organized crime, for that matter. Where are the glamour fights held? Las Vegas. Atlantic City. The casinos know that high-visibility fights bring in high-rolling customers. Naturally, there is a temptation to bend the odds in one's favor, which is why rumors of fight-fixing have always swirled around boxing. Some have been substantiated. Records are altered. The fighter with an advertised mark of 16-4 turns out to be a 7-12-1 bruiser, who only six days before the match was pumping gas in North Carolina. This happens more often than people might suspect.

In boxing's shark-infested waters, it pays to have good management. A patient, shrewd judge of talent can carry a fighter far. Rocky Graziano wasn't the world's most talented middleweight but he built his reputation by feasting on lean-and-hungry welterweights. Sugar Ray Leonard worked his way toward the welterweight championship by fighting nobodies, just as Marvelous Marvin Hagler was avoided for years by those at the top of the middleweight ranks. In 1987, Mark Breland, twenty-four, the undefeated Olympic gold medalist, lost his title to a journeyman welterweight named Marlon Starling. Breland had won 110 of 111 amateur bouts, won the world welterweight title in his seventeenth professional fight, and knocked out twelve straight fighters heading into his clash with Starling. But Breland's handlers lost that bout long before their boxer stepped in the ring because they hadn't prepared him gradually for a fighter of Starling's obvious skills. But, as Don King might say in an unguarded moment, let the buyer in boxing beware.

13

THE BOXERS

oxing has always been an egalitarian enterprise. From America's Jack Johnson to Germany's Max Schmeling to Italy's Primo Carnera to Sweden's Ingemar Johansson to Muhammad Ali, there has been only one requirement of world heavyweight champions: talent and a desire to win. Of course, the same is true of all weight classes.

Assembled here are a gallery of great fighters who overcame great odds to become champions. Consider Sugar Ray Leonard, who grew up in a well-heeled Baltimore suburb. He won the Olympic gold medal, then suffered the only loss of his career at the hands of Roberto Duran, the wickedly wonderful Panamanian. He triumphed in a welterweight rematch leaving Duran a broken man. Then there is Rocky Graziano, the hood who sharpened his skills at Stillman's Gym in New York. He wasn't the fanciest boxer, but he eventually escaped jail to win the middleweight crown from Tony Zale in 1947.

Here is Willie Pep, the overachieving featherweight who endured 242 lifetime bouts. There is heavyweight Rocky Marciano, a man who won all 49 of his professional bouts. Ezzard Charles was heavyweight champion as well, but he lost 25 of his 122 career bouts. Sugar Ray Robinson began his incredible welterweight career with a record of 123-1-2: Only a loss to Jake La Motta spoiled an otherwise perfect start. Cuba's Teofilio Stevenson is one of the greatest heavies of all time and he never fought professionally. Instead, three Olympic gold medals and two world amateur championships are his legacy.

Here are the greatest boxers ever—legends in their own time and for all time.

Rocky Marciano, seen here preparing for a 1950 fight with Roland La Starza, was one of only three undefeated heavyweight champions.

PHOTOWORLD/FPG Intl.

MUHAMMAD ALI

PHOTOWORLD/FPG Intl.

Heavyweight 56-5 (37 KO)

He transcended boxing, and so made it even greater. Cassius Marcellus Clay, Jr., later Muhammad Ali, floated like a butterfly and stung like a bee—and he told you about it, again and again. His mouth was easily more lethal than his jab or his left hook. He danced, he shucked, he jived. But there was more to Ali than mere charisma. He wasn't the greatest, as he liked to say, but Ali was truly one of history's best heavyweights.

Ali was born in Louisville, Kentucky on January 17, 1942. He won the honor of representing the United States at the 1960 Olympics in Rome and proceeded to box his way through the light heavyweight division. He outpointed Poland's Zbigniew Pietrzykowski for the gold medal and, naturally, predicted big things for himself. His first real chance to put his fists where his mouth was came on February 25, 1964 against heavyweight champion Sonny Liston.

The odds against Clay winning (this was his only title fight under that name) were eight to one. Liston was coming off of two consecutive one-round knockouts of former champion Floyd Patterson and seemed invincible. The fight doctor, a man named Robbin, would have agreed, based on his pre-fight examination of Ali. "He is emotionally unbalanced," Robbin said. "He acts like a man in mortal fear of death. Judging by his pulse rate, he's burning up energy at an enormous rate." Liston, however, was the one burned up, in a fight that ended when the champion could not rise from his stool for the sixth round. Ali's second knockout of Liston, in the first round, on May 25, 1965 in Lewiston, Maine certified his greatness.

There was no doubt: Ali was the greatest—and the prettiest, as he liked to say.
Even with a crowd of cameras looking on, Ali couldn't resist one last look in the mirror.

"I am the Greatest."

Ali first splashed on the scene in 1960, when he won the light heavyweight Olympic gold medal in Rome. Here, he is flanked by fellow winners middleweight Edward Crook, right, and light middleweight Wilbert McClure. Ali lost to Leon Spinks early in 1978, below, only to win the heavyweight title back seven months later; the heavyweight title passed to Larry Holmes in 1980 when he defeated Ali.

Ali, using a brutal combination of speed and power, defended his title nine times, beating boxers such as Patterson, Ernie Terrell, and Zora Folley. The Folley fight, on March 22, 1967, was Ali's last title fight for four years. He was stripped of his title in 1967 because he declined to enlist in the Army for religious reasons. Joe Frazier and Jimmy Ellis moved in and won the heavyweight championships while Ali bided his time. He returned to the ring on March 8, 1971 and fought Frazier in the first of three rousing bouts. Ali lost on points over fifteen rounds, but clearly reestablished himself as a fighting force. Two years later, George Foreman lifted the title from Frazier in Kingston, Jamaica with a stunning second-round knockout.

On October 30, 1974 Ali became only the second man in history to regain the heavyweight championship with an eight-round knockout of Foreman in Kinshasa, Zaire. Ali used defensive tactics to save his energy in the oppressive heat, then unleashed a series of furious punches. Thus, he had equaled Patterson's feat of again rising to the top. After three undistinguished defenses against Chuck Wepner, Ron Lyle, and Joe Bugner, Ali stopped Frazier in the fourteenth round of a celebrated October 1, 1975 fight. Another round of defenses against mediocre challengers led to Ali's upset by the raw Leon Spinks.

Ali was oddly flat against the young fighter in Las Vegas on February 18, 1978. Spinks took a well-deserved fifteen-round decision, upsetting Ali's try for a record—three world heavyweight titles. On September 15, 1978, Ali took back the title with a complete display of boxing. He swarmed Spinks, taking advantage of a sloppy defense and an uncertain offense. Ali, skills eroded, would lose the title to Larry Holmes in 1980, yet he was still a media event all by himself. He influenced a generation of fighters, who mimicked his verbal assaults on opponents and his clever poems. Those who studied his boxing style, however, benefited even more. Ali used the ring intelligently, and was adept at drawing an opponent's lead then moving his head maddeningly out of reach and following with a flurry of counter punches.

History, it is hoped, will equally regard Ali's compelling style and memorable substance.

© H.P. Brown/FPG Intl.

19

The Triple Champion

HENRY ARMSTRONG

PHOTOWORLD/FPG Intl.

Featherweight, welterweight, lightweight 145-20-9 (98 KO)

There have been many boxers who won two different titles—from Canadian bantamweight/featherweight George Dixon in the 1890s to Hector Camacho, a present-day lightweight. Beating a man in a higher weight class is the mark of truly committed and talented fighter. It requires a combination of gifts and guile.

What then to make of those men who aspire to the supreme challenge of stepping up two weight classes? The roster of three weight-class champions is a short one; only eight men managed the feat. Bob Fitzsimmons of Great Britain was the first to do it, winning middleweight, heavyweight, and light heavyweight titles between 1891 and 1903. The United State's Tony Canzoneri came along twenty-five years later and repeated the unlikely trilogy: featherweight (1928), lightweight (1930), and welterweight

(1931). Barney Ross of the United States followed with the lightweight title in 1933, light welterweight in the same year, and welterweight in 1934. And then came Henry Armstrong, who would redefine the role of triple champion forever.

Between October 1937 and August 1938 there was no one better in the featherweight, welterweight, and lightweight divisions than Henry Armstrong. For one year, no man who weighed between 122 and 142 pounds could beat him. Armstrong, in fact, was the only man in history to simultaneously hold three titles.

"Homicide Hank" was born in Columbus, Mississippi and left home at the age of nineteen for Los Angeles, California, where he became a successful amateur boxer. His first professional fight, in 1931, left him out cold on the canvas. Melody Jackson, as Armstrong called himself then, had suffered the first of only two

Henry Armstrong, the former world featherweight, welterweight, and lightweight champion has been rated as one of the best fighters, pound-for-pound, that the ring has ever known. Later, Reverend Armstrong, above, carried the fight to a higher plane.

knockouts in a career that spanned fifteen years. On October 29, 1937, Armstrong knocked out Petey Sarron in the sixth round of their New York fight to win the featherweight title. Ross, the most recent three-time champion of the day, lost his welterweight championship to Armstrong on May 31, 1938 in a fifteen-round decision at New York's Madison Square Bowl. On August 7, 1938, Armstrong took the lightweight title from Lou Ambers in a terrific bout that ended with a fifteen-round split decision.

Armstrong failed to make the featherweight limit ever again and lost the lightweight title to Ambers in a contest that ended a string of 47 victorious bouts. As a welterweight, however, he was untouchable. Between the Ross fight and September, 1940, Armstrong made nineteen consecutive title defenses in twenty-eight months. Only heavyweights Joe Louis (twenty-five) and Larry Holmes (twenty) ever produced more. Yet it wasn't Armstrong's durability that was so amazing—it was the frequency with which he accepted title fights.

Consider this five fight streak: October 9, 1939, Armstrong knocks out Al Manfredo in the fourth round; October 13, 1939, Armstrong knocks out Howard Scott in the second round; October 20, 1939, Armstrong knocks out Ritchie Fontaine in the third round; October 24, 1939, Armstrong decisions Jimmy Garrison in ten rounds; October 30, 1939, Armstrong knocks out Bobby Pacho in the fourth round. Five championship bouts, five victories, four knockouts—all in one month. From 1937 to 1941, Armstrong appeared in twenty-six world title fights, second only to Louis' twenty-seven.

Armstrong had great speed and was always on the attack. His feat of three simultaneous titles may never be broken. Incredibly, he very nearly won the middleweight crown during that period. Armstrong fought Ceferino Garcia to a ten-round draw in Los Angeles; a title must be won if a boxer is to be the new champion. Undoubtedly, Henry Armstrong understood. He knew something about being a champion.

EZZARD CHARLES

PHOTOWORLD/FPG Intl.

Heavyweight 96-25-1 (58 KO)

Critics said Ezzard Charles was in the right place at the right time; that he was fortunate to dominate the heavyweight landscape in the late 1940s and early 1950s, between the reigns of Joe Louis and Rocky Marciano.

Certainly, Charles became the champion by beating Jersey Joe Walcott, then thirty-five, and consolidated his title by bruising a thirty-six-year-old Louis, but Charles was a boxer at heart and he simply fought the man they placed in front of him. Charles fought a lot; he appeared in 122 professional fights – more than any heavyweight champion in history. The frequency with which he defended his title was staggering.

Charles was born on July 7, 1921 in Lawrenceville, Georgia. While he was growing up, Louis was the era's dominant boxer. He took the heavyweight championship from James J. Braddock in 1937 and held the title for nearly twelve years. On June 25, 1948, Louis knocked out Walcott in the eleventh round for his record twenty-fifth consecutive successful defense. And then he retired. It was decided that Walcott and Charles, a promising heavyweight living in Cincinnati, Ohio, would fight for Louis' vacated title.

On June 22, 1949, in the same Chicago ring that Louis had dethroned Braddock for the championship—twelve years earlier to the day—Charles met Walcott. Walcott was nearly eight years older than Charles, but he enjoyed a fourteen-pound advantage over him. Charles, an even six feet tall, weighed but 182 pounds, only seven pounds above the light heavyweight limit. Still, his punches carried a deceptive power.

From the beginning, Charles threw body shots that rocked Walcott, who answered with a series of wild right hands that failed

In 1949, Charles focused on his upcoming heavyweight fight with Joe Walcott,
as business manager Jean Elkins watched from the shadows.

Durable Champion

to find the mark. On three different occasions (the seventh, tenth, and eleventh rounds), Charles seemed to have the older fighter on the verge of a knockout. It went fifteen rounds, though, and amid a chorus of boos from the spectators, Charles was awarded the obvious decision. Louis was the first to congratulate Charles. "Walcott never changed his style," Louis observed. "Ezzard had to force the fight all the way. He deserved to win." So moved by Charles' effort was manager Jake Mintz, that he collapsed in the corner when Charles was declared the new champion.

Today, with so much money at stake, heavyweight champions are reluctant to defend their precious titles very often. In those days, there was less on the line and, besides, Charles had always been a busy fighter. Less than two months after winning the title, Charles was back in the ring against Gus Lesnevich in New York. The referee stopped the fight in the seventh round. Pat Velentino was a knockout victim two months later, and Freddy Beshore was Charles' third defense victim. On September 27, 1950, Charles faced Louis himself.

PHOTOWORLD/FPG Intl.

The "Brown Bomber" had lost only once before (to Max Schmeling in 1936) but this time he hadn't been in the ring for eighteen months. Louis fought creditably enough, sending Charles back on his heels with a brutal left hook in the fourth round. In the tenth, Louis stunned and staggered Charles, bloodying his nose. The Yankee Stadium crowd jumped to its feet, but Charles, seven years younger, weathered the storm. He battered and bloodied Louis over fifteen rounds and was declared the winner on points.

Charles would defend his undisputed title four more times in the next eight months, before running into Walcott for the third time. Charles was knocked out in the seventh round and never again challenged for the title. However, his eight successful title defenses over a nineteen month span were unprecedented for a heavyweight champion.

Charles didn't have a heavy muscular physique like Jersey Joe Walcott, but he prevailed in their 1949 championship bout.

Boxing Comes to the Masses

JACK
DEMPSEY

Heavyweight 62-6-10 (49 KO)

Unquestionably, Jack Dempsey was one of history's best-loved heavyweights. He also happened to be one of the best.

"The Champ" first began capturing imaginations in the Roaring Twenties, before boxing had established itself as a favorite sport among Americans. In Toledo, Ohio he had won the heavyweight title in patriotic fashion on July 4, 1919, stopping Jess Willard in three rounds. Some people were upset, however, when Dempsey avoided military service during World War I, and promoters used his less-than-heroic image to their advantage. On July 2, 1921, Dempsey knocked out Frenchman Georges Carpentier in the fourth round, and the well-staged fight grossed $1.7 million—a first for boxing. It was the first world title fight to be broadcast over the radio in its entirety. Dempsey defended his title twice more before a bout with Luis "Angel" Firpo catapulted him into the national spotlight.

It was probably the most devastating heavyweight fight of all time. On September 14, 1923, Dempsey knocked down the "Wild Bull of the Pampas" nine times in the first round alone. At the same time, one of the South American's punches took Dempsey right out of the ring. In round two, Dempsey sent Firpo to the canvas twice before he stayed down for good. Those eleven knockdowns were surpassed only once in a title fight—by bantamweight Vic Toweel, in a 1950 fight with Danny O. Sullivan. Quite naturally, Dempsey developed a reputation as a brawling, heroic figure. The rewards were staggering: in 1924 alone, Dempsey took home more than a $500,000 from boxing exhibitions and movie roles. Today, that amount is worth more than $10 million.

As Dempsey prepared for a 1930 bout against Jack Sharkey, the sand bag spoke volumes about his punching power.

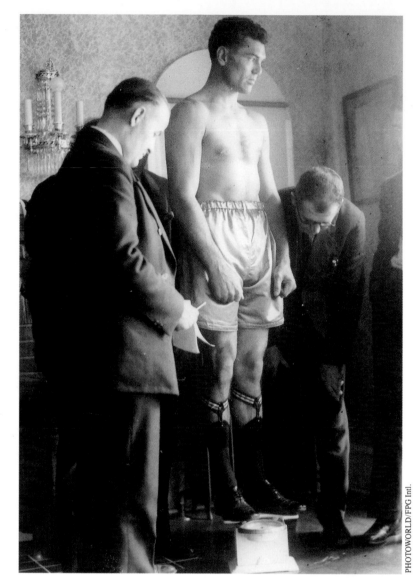

*The heavyweight champion bared his soul—and his garters—during this Atlantic City weigh-in. Even without the leather gloves, **right**, Dempsey looked impressive in the gym.*

And the fascination didn't abate with the Firpo bout. On September 23, 1926, Dempsey met Gene Tunney at Philadelphia's Sesquicentennial Stadium, with 120,757 in the seats. That represented the first live gate to exceed one million dollars, and what a fight the fans saw. Tunney ended Dempsey's seven year, eighty-one day reign as heavyweight champion with a ten-round decision. A year later, Tunney successfully defended his title against Dempsey before a crowd of 104,943 at Chicago's Soldier Field. Dempsey managed a seventh-round knockdown, but Tunney survived the famed "long count" and recovered to win another ten-round decision. Dempsey retired immediately. Yet, he had personally vaulted boxing from a dubious enterprise to a professional sport second only to baseball in popularity.

Dempsey was born in Manassa, Colorado on June 24, 1893 as William Harrison Dempsey. By 1914, he was fighting under the name of "Kid Blackie" but borrowed a new name, Jack, when his older brother died. They both admired erstwhile middleweight champion Jack Dempsey, and hoped the name would bring them similar luck. In young William's case, the change did just that. Manager Jack Kearns came along in 1917 and polished Dempsey's crude power into the tools of a dangerous fighting machine.

By now, Dempsey had become known as the "Manassa Mauler." His third-round knockout of Jess Willard was the first glimpse of what he was capable of. At 6 feet, 192 pounds, Dempsey was five inches and nearly sixty pounds smaller than his opponent. Still, he won the title—though Kearns had wagered the entire winning purse at ten-to-one odds that Dempsey would win by a first-round knockout. The prize money and the knockouts, however, were just beginning.

Dempsey chose to earn his money in exhibitions, rather than frequent title defenses. When he retired in 1940, he had taken in more than ten million dollars. And, of his 49 career knockouts, 25 came in the first round.

EMILE GRIFFITH

85-24-2 (23 KO)
Welterweight, middleweight

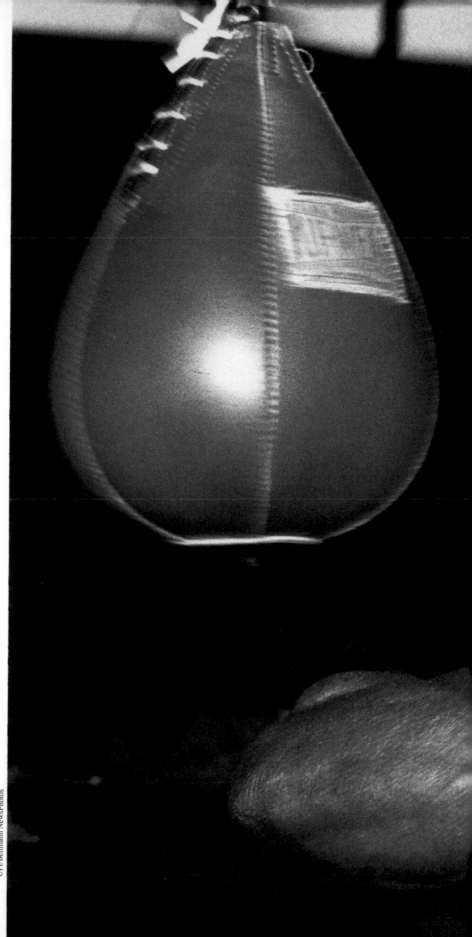

Emile Griffith was forever young, or so it looked when he practiced his craft in the boxing ring. When he began his career as a promising welterweight in 1958, Dwight D. Eisenhower was the president of the United States. And Griffith was still fighting in 1977 when Jimmy Carter occupied the Oval Office.

Griffith was born in the Virgin Islands, and as he grew older a job as an apprentice hatmaker seemed to loom in his future. But by the age of twenty, he had relocated to New York City and become a Golden Gloves champion. In March of 1960, a ten round decision over Denny Moyer effectively stamped him as a welterweight contender.

On April Fool's Day, 1961, Griffith stepped into the ring against Cuban champion Benny Paret in Miami, and proved he wasn't joking. In only his twenty-fourth professional fight, Griffith floored Paret with a brutal right hand, and the title was his. There was a successful defense two months later, when Griffith stopped Mexico's Gaspar "Indian" Ortega in Los Angeles. On September 30, 1961, Paret won his crown back with a fifteen-round decision in New York. That set up an ill-fated rubber match that lives today in infamy.

New York was the site of the trumpeted rematch and both fighters delivered on the great expectations. However, toward the later rounds Griffith's strength began to show. In the twelfth round he battered Paret's face into a swollen mass of blood. The referee stopped the fight and Griffith again was champion, while Paret was taken to the hospital with massive brain damage. He died ten days later and public sentiment at the time forced Griffith to briefly withdraw from the ring.

Emile Griffith, in a classic pose, was anything but a classic fighter. At the age of thirty, he had won five world titles and lost only eight bouts. He spent the next ten years trying to capture the elusive sixth championship belt.

UPI/Bettmann NewsPhotos

Spirit of Youth

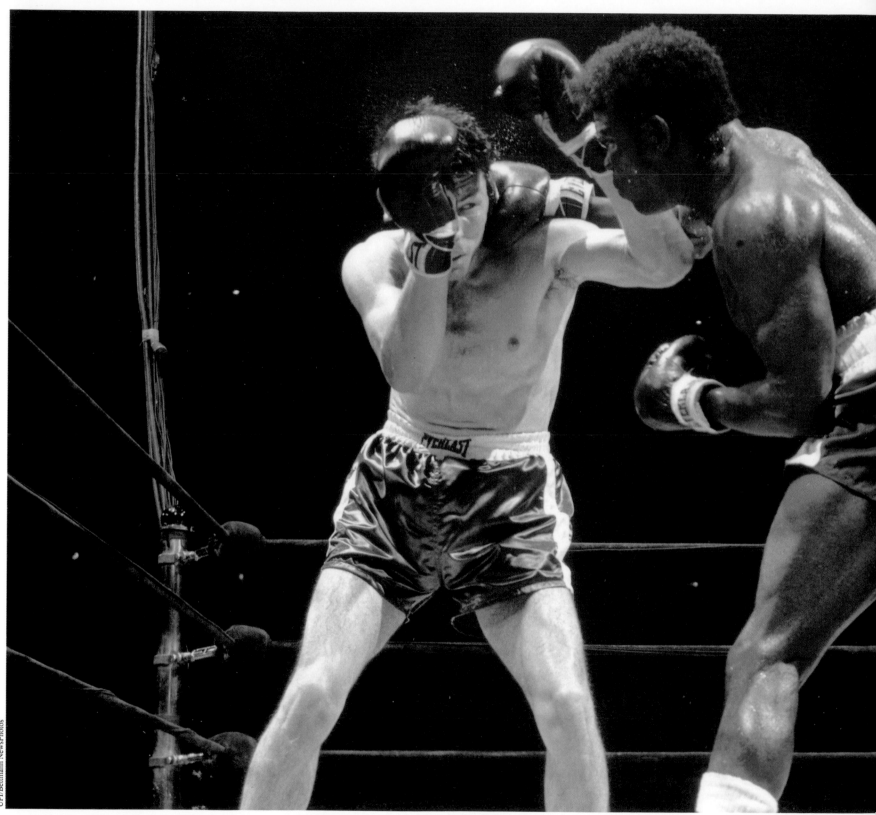

Griffith, the middleweight champion, sweated out a fifteen-round decision over challenger Joey Archer in 1966.

His resiliency, evident in this third fight against Paret, carried Griffith through two more defenses before Cuba's Luis Rodriguez lifted the title. Three months later, Griffith's fifteen-round decision gave him back the championship for the third time. Griffith beat Rodriguez again one year later.

In 1965, Griffith moved up to middleweight but lost in his maiden voyage to champion Don Fulmer. A year later, Griffith succeeded against Dick Tiger for his fourth title and gave up his welterweight crown. In 1967, Griffith lost the middleweight championship to Italy's Nino Benvenuti, but recouped five months later to become champion for a fifth time. On March 4, 1968, Griffith surrendered the title to Benvenuti in the first world title fight at the new Madison Square Garden.

At the age of thirty, Griffith had lost only eight bouts. He would spend the next ten years trying to win that elusive sixth title and lose sixteen fights in the process—not that he wasn't a serious contender. In 1969, Griffith returned to the welterweight division and lost on points in a fifteen-round decision to champion Jose Napoles. Two years later, Griffith lost in fourteen rounds to middleweight champ Carlos Monzon. In 1973, Monzon outlasted Griffith for a narrow fifteen-round decision. His last fight, at the age of thirty-nine, came against Britain's Alan Minter. Griffith lost in ten rounds and opted for retirement.

Later, Griffith became a respected trainer, a role that allowed him to pass his knowledge along to a stable of contenders. His ageless example was always a source of motivation and pride. "They help keep me young," Griffith once said of his protégés. Clearly, he didn't need much help.

True Grit

ROCKY GRAZIANO

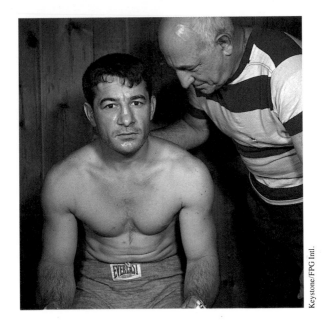

Keystone/FPG Intl.

Middleweight 67-10-6 (52 KO)

To be frank, Rocky Graziano was not the world's greatest middleweight. Sure, he was the champion for nearly eleven months, but that was only a brief interlude during the reign of Tony Zale. And though Graziano's ring record of 67-10-6 was better than Zale's 67-18-2, there was no question that Zale was the more accomplished fighter. But when a boxer becomes the stuff of legends his success is not always based strictly on talent. Graziano's forte was survival. He is one of the best examples of boxing's egalitarian nature, and showed that anyone with a thirst for the championship could succeed, despite the odds.

It was boxing that rescued Graziano from a life of crime. He grew up on New York's East Side with the rather extraordinary name of Thomas Rocco Barbella. Soon it was just Rocky—and

that was an adequate description of his early life. He was a tough kid who spent a fair amount of time in jails around the greater New York area. His heroes were the gangsters who carried guns and flaunted the law on a regular basis. Even as he matured, Graziano's character remained dubious.

He was drafted into the Army, but walked out in favor of Stillman's gym to resume his boxing careeer. When an Army lieutenant confronted the deserter with a few pointed questions, Graziano dropped him with a right cross. Eventually, the Army won out and Graziano did some time in a military stockade before he returned to the ring.

Graziano's boxing career began in 1942, and his managers guided him well. The majority of his early fights were against smaller welterweights. On September 27, 1946, Graziano met

Middleweight Rocky Graziano lost 10 of his 83 career bouts, but his occasional lack of substance was overcome by a rakish style in the ring.

Graziano's right hand was a constant threat to the well-being of Tony Zale's face. That right hand paid Graziano's bills.

Tony Zale for the first of three memorable fights. Zale was in many ways opposite to Graziano. He had first won the middle-weight title from Al Hostak in 1940 with a thirteenth-round knockout. Zale successfully defended his championship title three times before joining the Navy, where he served, agreeably, for four years. The championship fight against Graziano at Yankee Stadium was the first important open air fight after the war ended. It did much to recycle enthusiasm into the sport.

For the first five rounds, Zale looked like a man who hadn't fought a championship fight in more than five years. But in the sixth round, Zale found the old form and hit Graziano with a right to the chest, followed by a left hook to the jaw. One more left hook left Graziano crumpled in the middle of the ring. It was a sixth-round knockout and the ferocity of the fight made a rematch nec-essary. In Chicago, on July 16, 1947, Graziano whipped Zale with his own sixth-round knockout. It was intolerably hot inside the arena, and Zale hung on the ropes as Graziano stormed him with body shots. The referee was moved to stop the fight, but Zale claimed it was premature. Nevertheless, Graziano was the cham-pion. On July 10, 1948, Zale returned the favor with a third-round knockout at Newark, New Jersey. Those fights defined the ring career of Rocky Graziano.

As all three of his fights with Zale produced six-figure gates, Graziano was set for life. He became a wildly popular personality and made an easy transition from boxing to television. He wrote a book, "Somebody Up There Likes Me", and appeared in movies. The title of his autobiography expressed it best; without question, Graziano went farther with less, than any boxer of his era.

MARVELOUS MARVIN HAGLER

© Mike Valeri/FPG Intl.

Middleweight 62-3-2 (52 KO)

He is the classic fighter; a man wronged early, and often, in life; a man who holds to his internal deep fury even when opportunity rises to greet him. Marvelous Marvin Hagler, a devastating punching machine, unleashed his anger in three minute doses and it made him one of the world's great middleweights.

Born in Newark, New Jersey on May 23, 1954, Hagler eventually landed in Brockton, Massachusetts, where he fought as an amateur. In the 1973 National AAU Tournament, Hagler was named the most valuable boxer. In that same competition, Randy Shields beat a boxer named Sugar Ray Leonard. Leonard chose the Olympic route in 1976 and became an overnight television hero. When Leonard turned professional, his debut bout offered a forty thousand dollar prize. Hagler, meanwhile, earned fifty dol-

lars for winning his first professional fight, and ten of that hefty prize went for registration.

Hagler fought in obscurity, honing his craft quietly in the shadow of middleweight champion Carlos Monzon. Potential titlists avoided Hagler and his brawling, unorthodox style. He was a dangerous in-fighter who liked to butt heads with opponents to see how tough they were. In the thirty-sixth fight of his career, Hagler fought on the undercard for fifteen hundred dollars, while Leonard's third fight as a professional was the card's fifty thousand dollar main event.

With a state legislator's help, Hagler got his first title shot on November 30, 1979. He was already twenty-five and had been a worthy contender for more than four years. In this, his fiftieth career bout, Hagler made forty thousand dollars. Incredibly, that

The gleaming shaved head. The defiant look. It was all part of Marvelous Marvin Hagler's way of remembering the bad times, his obscure life before he was finally permitted to try for the middleweight title in 1979.

Angry Underdog Triumphant

In 1979, Marvin Hagler failed to beat middleweight champion Vito Antuofermo in a bloody fifteen-round draw. Two years later, Hagler retired Antuofermo in four rounds.

night, Leonard was again the main event as he defeated Wilfred Benitez for the World Boxing Council welterweight title. It only added to Hagler's general misery when he outboxed Vito Antuofermo, left his face a mask of blood, but failed to win the championship when the judges called the fight a controversial draw.

Alan Minter of Great Britain took the title Hagler hungered for by decisioning Antuofermo over fifteen rounds a year later. Antuofermo was an eighth-round knockout victim in the rematch a year later. Finally, on September 27, 1980, Hagler became champion. He had placed himself in isolation for training, as he always did. In solitary confinement at the far end of Cape Cod, Massachusetts, Hagler pushed himself to the limit, shaved head gleaming, bicep muscles blurring as he hit the speed bag. This time, there was no draw. The referee stopped the London fight in the third round and the eternal underdog had been delivered.

Hagler wore his championship well. He defended the title twelve times, two short of Monzon's middleweight record. There was a convincing fourth-round knockout of Antuofermo and a pair of knockouts over Venezuela's Fulgencio Obelmejias. Roberto Duran loomed on the horizon and Hagler decisioned him in a cautious fight. The key to Hagler's attack was a random aggression that barely resembled boxing. Yet it was an April 15, 1985 fight in Las Vegas (his signature bout) that will always linger in the minds of those who saw it. In that fight, Hagler systematically destroyed Thomas Hearns in three rounds and, for the first time, established himself as one of the world's greatest fighters. He followed that with an eleventh-round knockout of John "The Beast" Mugabi, a boxer who had knocked out all of his twenty six previous opponents. After that fight, only one possibility loomed for Hagler, and that was Leonard. Hagler, who remembered all the old injustices, demanded a purse of twelve million dollars when he learned Leonard would make eleven million. He got his way—and the fight of his life.

Hagler had not lost in nearly eleven years. But, on April 6, 1987, Leonard outboxed him and won a close twelve-round decision. Some observers felt that Hagler had actually won the fight, that Leonard was all flash and dash. For Hagler, who had held the middleweight title for nearly seven years, it was nothing new. Still, while he was on top, there wasn't a better fighter in the world.

Street Fighting Man

THOMAS
HEARNS

© Lisa O'Connor/Ron Galella Ltd.

Welterweight, super welterweight, middleweight, light heavyweight, 45-2 (38 KO)

In another time, Thomas Hearns might be hailed as one of history's greatest fighters pound-for-pound. It was his misfortune that he shared weight classes and an era with ageless legends Sugar Ray Leonard and Marvin Hagler. Both beat Hearns in celebrated conflicts that generated millions of dollars and captured the public's limited boxing imagination of the 1980s. This should not be held against him.

Born on October 18, 1958 in Detroit, Michigan, Hearns was a skinny kid who suffered at the hands of the neighborhood toughs. When he got tired of the abuse, Hearns joined the King Solomon Gym. Self-defense was his primary motivation, but Hearns actually liked to fight. Soon, he moved to the Kronk Gym; it was there that he met Manual Steward. "I've never seen anybody, ever, who had no fear of nobody," said Steward, the man who turned a vio-

lent youth into a world champion. "But Tommy didn't then, and he doesn't now."

Hearns won 155 amateur bouts and was named 1977's outstanding amateur boxer. He won the national AAU and Golden Gloves championships. Clearly, Hearns was something special. They were already calling him the "Motor City Cobra" and "Hit Man" when he turned professional in November, 1977. With Steward choosing his early bouts with care, Hearns won his first 17 fights—all by knockout. In 1980, Pipino Cuevas was the World Boxing Association's welterweight champion, but Hearns took the title from him with a crushing second-round knockout. After three successful defenses, Hearns signed to fight Leonard.

It was billed as "The Showdown" and it truly lived up to its billing. Leonard, the popular World Boxing Council champion,

The two faces of Thomas Hearns: The classic street fighter, left, *and the confident welterweight, super welterweight, middleweight, and light heavyweight champ,* above.

Before he won his record fourth title, Hearns, right, suffered the wrath of Marvin Hagler. He lost the bout to Hagler after eight of boxing's most savage minutes.

was the favorite. He was engaging and a familiar sight on the nation's televisions, hawking soda pop and other products. Hearns, at 6-feet, 1-inch, usually wore a menacing look that didn't translate into endorsements. It worked just fine in the ring, though.

On September 16, 1981, Hearns outboxed Leonard for most of thirteen rounds. His long reach, effective jab, and murderous body shots gave him the lead on the judges' cards. Then, in the fourteenth round, Leonard's greatness emerged. He summoned a flurry of punches and knocked a dazed Hearns into the ropes. That was the first loss of Hearns' career.

Even in defeat, Hearns had won praise as a multi-dimensional fighter. On December 3, 1982, he rallied and won a fifteen-round decision from Wilfred Benitez for the WBC super welterweight crown. Hearns was successful in three title defenses, including a devastating second-round knockout of former Panamanian champion Roberto Duran. That result led to a fight with Hagler, the reigning middleweight champion. For Hearns it was a chance for his third title, something only eight boxers had previously managed. Some doubted that Hearns could fight effectively at 160 pounds, but his large frame and effort against Duran eased those fears.

In the end, Hearns' courage—as Steward said, he wasn't afraid of anyone—was his downfall. As Leonard would later prove in his masterful twelve-round decision over Hagler, finesse is the key to success against Hearns. There is nothing delicate about Hearns and he made a fatal decision to trade punches with Hagler. In one of the most brutal eight minutes in boxing history, Hagler tore Hearns apart. Sadly, the memory of Hearns lying prone in the Las Vegas ring is the one that lingers. After the second loss of his career, Hearns made another comeback. First, he took the WBC light heavyweight title. Then, when he knocked out Roldan in Las Vegas for his unprecedented fourth title, Hearns' destiny had been fulfilled.

LARRY HOLMES

© Victor Aleman/FPG Intl.

Heavyweight 48-3 (34 KO)

He was dogged by critics who said he wasn't a devastating puncher, that the lack of competition in the heavyweight division left him a paper champion. Larry Holmes wasn't as dazzling as Muhammad Ali—after all, who was?—and as a result, he never received the attention and credit he deserved.

Look at that career record: 48-3. That means Holmes won ninety-six percent of his bouts, including the first 48. He fell one short of Rocky Marciano's glittering 49-0 record in a bid to complete his career as one of only four undefeated champions. And Holmes didn't miss by much. On September 20, 1985, he lost a fifteen-round decision to Michael Spinks in Las Vegas and promptly retired. He came out of retirement just as quickly and lost a second fight to Spinks. On January 22, 1988 Holmes again

came out of retirement to fight Mike Tyson. In a fight which was obviously meant to be his last, Holmes earned 3 million dollars for the less-than-twelve minutes it took for Tyson to knock him out. It was an unfitting end to a marvelous career.

Holmes was born on November 3, 1949 in Cuthbert, Georgia. One of a sharecropper's eleven children, he quickly learned how to survive under difficult circumstances. Despite his physical talent—Holmes was 6-foot-3, 225 pounds—he was not regarded as a contender for the heavyweight title, at least not initially. He turned professional in 1973 and took jobs as a sparring partner for both Ali and Joe Frazier as they dueled for the heavyweight championship in the mid-70s.

Finally, on June 10, 1978, Holmes got his first title shot. Ken Norton was the champ at the time, having been proclaimed the top

Holmes didn't need a benediction from wild-haired promoter Don King, above, or cornerman Richie Giachetti. He won the first forty-eight fights of his professional career, one of the best heavyweight marks in history.

The Sparring Partner

50

In the 1970s, Holmes was lucky to land a job as Muhammad Ali's sparring partner. In 1980, Holmes mastered his former employer in a fight that ended after ten rounds.

heavyweight three months earlier. Holmes beat Norton on points over fifteen rounds in Las Vegas and his record climbed to 28-0. Holmes had one of history's best left jabs and enough power in either hand to take opponents out with ease.

After winning the title, Holmes went on to defend his championship belt twenty times. Only Joe Louis' record of twenty-five is higher for fighters in any weight classification. The roster of those champions who follow Holmes in the record book with nineteen successful defenses is instructive: Ali, welterweight Henry Armstrong, bantamweight Manual Ortiz, and featherweight Eusebio Perdroza.

Holmes' seven-year, one hundred and four-day reign included fights against any and all challengers, some good, some horribly bad. There was a seventh-round knockout against the awkward Alfredo Evangelista and brief encounters with boxers named Ossie Ocasio, Lorenzo Zanon, and Leroy Jones. On October 2, 1980, Holmes handled his former employer, Ali, stopping him in the tenth round. The vision of Ali, a slumping, tired, and thirty-eight year-old fighter, only contributed to the perception that there really was no competition out there for Holmes.

As he grew older, his victories became less definitive. Reynaldo Snipes hurt Holmes for the first time in his career before exiting in the eleventh round of their 1981 fight. Gerry Cooney, a fighter of questionable heart, lasted thirteen rounds with Holmes on June 12, 1982. Five months later, Randall "Tex" Cobb, whose boxing skills were never evident, nevertheless went fifteen rounds before losing the decision. There were similarly disappointing efforts against James "Bonecrusher" Smith and David Bey before Holmes won his twentieth defense against Carl "The Truth" Williams. It was a difficult fifteen-round decision for Holmes, who looked every day of his thirty-five years.

Meanwhile, Spinks had been roaring through the light heavyweight ranks and, looking for a new challenge, accepted a bout with Holmes. By then, it was clear Holmes had overstayed his welcome, and overreached his ability. He lost to Spinks in that 1985 fight and later lost a rematch. Still, Holmes should be remembered as the champion who won his first 48 bouts, rather than the boxer who lost his last three.

America's Sweetheart

SUGAR RAY LEONARD

Newsworld/FPG Intl.

Welterweight, light middleweight, middleweight 34-1 (24 KO)

From the very beginning, Sugar Ray Leonard was the best and the brightest. Born Ray Charles Leonard on May 17, 1956 in Palmer Park, Maryland, it wasn't long before his ring talent invited comparison with Sugar Ray Robinson, the stylish middleweight. Everything Leonard touched turned to gold. He won a gold medal at the Montreal Olympics in 1976, defeating Cuba's Andres Aldama for the light welterweight title. His professional career was nothing short of spectacular.

Playing on the publicity and good will generated by his Olympic performance, Leonard collected forty-thousand dollars for his first fight. The hometown hero decisioned Luis Vega in Baltimore and immediately went on to bigger and better things. Less than three years later, Leonard was the champion of the world. He was charming, quicker than light, and packed some power behind his

blinding punches. Leonard outboxed Wilfred Benitez in Las Vegas on November 30, 1979, stopping him with six seconds left in the bout. The celebrated draw between Vito Antuofermo and Marvin Hagler for the middleweight title was on the same card.

Even as Leonard was defending his title against Dave Green, the critics were mistaking his nifty ringmanship and good looks for a lack of killer instinct. On June 20, 1980 they thought they had the evidence they were looking for. That night, Leonard lost a fifteen-round decision to Duran (his first loss as a professional) who brawled past him on the site of his Olympic triumph. But those detractors were far from the mark. Five months later at the Superdome in New Orleans, Leonard summoned the strength to leave the famed "Manos de Piedras" quivering and confused in his corner. A mature Leonard, at the height of his power, dodged

Do not be fooled by the cherubic exterior—certainly, Leonard's opponents weren't. He was slick and stylish, and later fights with Hagler and Hearns proved that this "Sugar" wasn't all sweetness.

The world discovered Leonard during the 1976 Summer Olympic games in Montreal; thee years later he was the professional welterweight champion of the world. With six seconds left in their title fight, Leonard Knocked out champion Wilfred Benitez, **right**, *in Las Vegas.*

Duran's wild overhand rights, stuck his tongue out at the champion, and wound up several times for exaggerated punches. In the eighth Duran waved his glove at Leonard in disgust and uttered the immortal words, "No mas. No mas."

With that, Leonard regained his World Boxing Council title. After defending it against Larry Bonds, Leonard stepped up to light middleweight and took the World Boxing Association championship from Ayub Kalule on June 5, 1981. That accomplished, Leonard relinquished the title for one reason—to train for a confrontation with Thomas Hearns, the WBA welterweight champion. On September 16, 1981, in Las Vegas, Leonard collected a then-record purse of eleven million dollars. Hearns had Leonard in trouble early in the bout, but Sugar Ray rallied. Although his face was horribly swollen, Leonard dropped Hearns to the canvas in the fourteenth round and became undisputed champion.

Leonard retired suddenly after a defense against Bruce Finch in early 1982. The champion had suffered a detached retina and doctors said a continued career in boxing was a threat to his eyesight. In 1984, Leonard chose to come back from surgery and fight Keven Howard, against the wishes of his wife, Juanita. Though he was knocked down for the first time in his career, Leonard struggled to win with a ninth-round knockout. Immediately after the fight, he announced his retirement—again.

This retirement was not to last. Marvin Hagler, the middleweight champion, was still available, and the prospect of an eleven-million-dollar payday lured Leonard into the ring. On April 6, 1987, Sugar Ray won a narrow, twelve-round decision from Hagler for his third different title, and the begrudging admiration of boxing's mainstream: This Sugar boxed as sweet as he looked.

JOE LOUIS

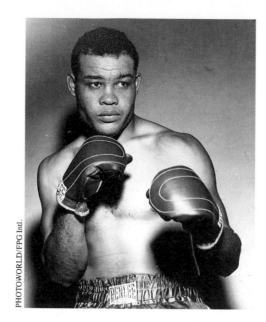

PHOTOWORLD/FPG Intl.

Heavyweight 63-3 (49 KO)

He was more than a fighter. Joe Louis was a symbol that black and white Americans could coexist. He was a role model for all Americans and a champion for all time.

Louis was the heavyweight champion from June 22, 1937 until March 1, 1949, a duration of eleven years and two-hundred and fifty-two days. Louis reigned longer than any other titleholder in history, and he did it in boxing's premier division.

Born on May 13, 1914 in a Lafayette, Alabama sharecropper's shack, Louis found himself, at the age of twenty, in Chicago under the care of trainer Jack Blackburn. At the time, he stood just over 6 feet and weighed only 175 pounds. Though he lacked polish, Louis had power to spare in his awkward lunges around the ring.

"You know, boy, the heavyweight division for a Negro is hardly likely," Blackburn, a former fighter who was also black, told Louis one day. "The white man ain't too keen on it. You have to be really something to get anywhere. The dice is loaded against you. You gotta knock 'em out and keep knocking 'em out to get anywheres. Let your right fist be the referee."

Louis rarely let a bout come down to someone else's decision. On July 19, 1936, Louis was a 218-pound undefeated fighter of twenty-two facing German Max Schmeling. The symbolic implications of the fight with Schmeling, which came at the height of Adolph Hitler's power, were not lost on Louis. "I won't let my people down," Louis said. Yet, Schmeling knocked him out in the twelfth round of their fight at Yankee Stadium. A fourth-round knockdown, foreshadowed the final roundhouse right that laid him to the canvas for good. Naturally, Hitler was delighted.

Trainer Manny Seamon held the heavy bag in place while
Louis trained for a fight later that year.

Champion For the Ages

Billy Conn, and Joe Louis never quite saw eye-to-eye. In this 1946 fight at Yankee Stadium, Louis won with an eighth-round knockout.

The "Brown Bomber," as the newspapermen patronizingly called him, didn't dwell long on his defeat. He knocked out Jack Sharkey in the third round of their fight a month later and would remain unbeaten for an incredible period of fifteen years. On June 22, 1937, Louis squared off against champion James Braddock in Chicago. With forty-five thousand people squeezed into Comiskey Park, Louis went down in the first round when Braddock found him with a right uppercut. But, in the eighth, exhausted by a steady dose of Louis' jabs, Braddock took a whistling overhand right to the head and crashed to the canvas. Louis was the heavyweight champion of the world, the youngest ever, and only the second black after Jack Johnson.

Exactly a year later, Schmeling got his comeuppance. It had taken a year of maneuvering by managers on both sides to bring off the bout, but now Louis and Schmeling would fight in front of seventy thousand spectators at Yankee Stadium. Though he had lost to Schmeling earlier, Louis wore a look of confidence. "I'm scared," he had told a friend earlier that day. "Scared I might kill Schmeling tonight." Louis was so worried, he slept for several hours in his dressing room just before the fight. Louis swarmed over Schmeling in the first round, breaking two of the vertabrae in his back at one point. A left hook and an overhand right finished Schmeling, who couldn't go down because his chin was caught on the ring's top rope.

In Louis' next twenty-five world title bouts, only three men— Tommy Farr, Jersey Joe Walcott, and Arturo Godoy—managed to go the distance with him. He was inactive during World War II, but returned in 1946 with an eighth-round knockout of Billy Conn. Louis lost for only the second time in his career in 1950, to Ezzard Charles on points, and retired in 1951 after Rocky Marciano knocked him out in the eighth round.

By then, Jackie Robinson had joined the Brooklyn Dodgers. The Supreme Court had rendered a decision in Brown vs. Board of Education. And Joe Louis was a legend. Yet he was never an outspoken critic of racism in America; that wasn't his style. His right hand was far more eloquent.

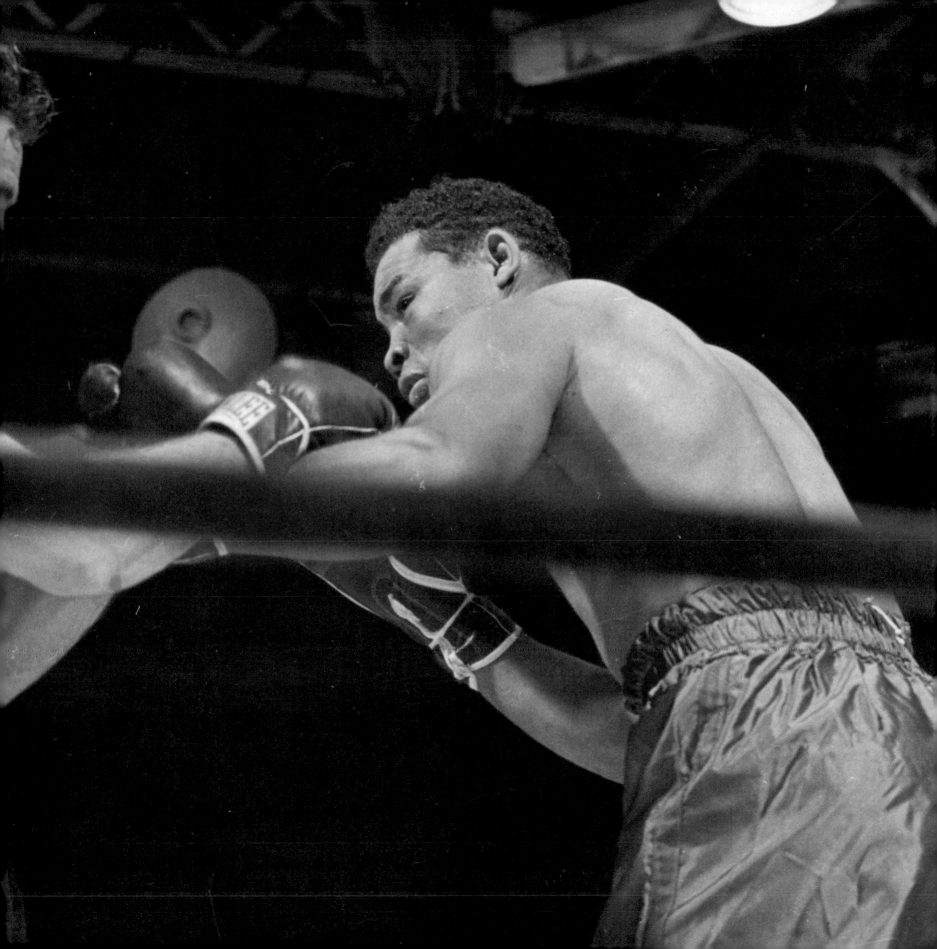

Perfection

ROCKY
MARCIANO

PHOTOWORLD/FPG Intl.

Heavyweight 49-0 (43 KO)

One of sport's tragedies is the athlete who lingers too long. His talent in twilight, he tries to relive past athletic glories for love, money, or simply because he doesn't know anything else. Rare is the sports hero who leaves on top, unmarred by the wars of competition. Jim Brown, the football player, comes to mind. Yet, perhaps Rocky Marciano is the best example.

Only three world champion boxers moved through their careers unscathed, and Marciano is the only one belonging to the twentieth century. Jim Barry of the United States, who fought as a bantamweight from 1891 to 1899, finished 59-0-9. Irish lightweight Jack McAuliffe was 41-0-9 from 1884 to 1897. Marciano never fought to a draw, winning all 49 of his professional fights—one of the truly great statistics in athletic achievement. And 43 of those fights ended in knockouts, one of boxing's great power ratios.

Rocco Francis Marchegiano was born in Brockton, Massachusetts on September 1, 1923. He came relatively late to the fighting game, taking his first professional bout at the age of twenty-four. Marciano served with the Untied States forces in Britain during World War II where he had some success as an amateur. He soon acquired the name of the "Brockton Blockbuster" but like later Brockton resident Marvelous Marvin Hagler, was denied access to a title fight for many years. Marciano was nearly thirty when manager Al Weill finally secured a contest with heavyweight champion Jersey Joe Walcott.

Marciano stood just under 5-foot-11 and weighed only 189 pounds, but his broad shoulders and bulky arms contained a power that belied his size. Perhaps it was his delayed arrival to

You would never know it to look at his battered face, but Rocky Marciano smiled for the cameras after he knocked out heavyweight champion Joe Walcott in their 1952 bout. **Left,** *Marciano strikes a more classic pose.*

boxing, or maybe it was the attitude he developed in his tough Massachusetts hometown. Whatever it was, on September 23, 1952, Marciano ripped into Walcott like a buzzsaw. At Philadelphia Stadium, he took the title from Walcott with a right-handed punch that separated the champion from his senses in the thirteenth round. It was one of the hardest punches Marciano ever threw and it established him as one of boxing's all-time sluggers.

A year earlier, Marciano had met Joe Louis in a fight that would prove to be the last of Louis' magnificent career. In the eighth round of their Madison Square Garden fight, Marciano caught Louis in the neck with a looping right that knocked him out of the ring. It was only the third loss in sixty-six bouts for Louis, and at the age of thirty-seven he had the good sense to retire.

Marciano's right hand developed a personality all its own and a name, too—"Suzi-Q." He gave Walcott a rematch in Chicago on

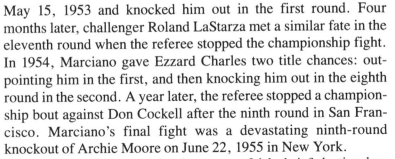

Walcott dropped Marciano in the first round of their 1952 title fight, but the challenger climbed off the canvas to record a thirteenth-round knockout.

May 15, 1953 and knocked him out in the first round. Four months later, challenger Roland LaStarza met a similar fate in the eleventh round when the referee stopped the championship fight. In 1954, Marciano gave Ezzard Charles two title chances: outpointing him in the first, and then knocking him out in the eighth round in the second. A year later, the referee stopped a championship bout against Don Cockell after the ninth round in San Francisco. Marciano's final fight was a devastating ninth-round knockout of Archie Moore on June 22, 1955 in New York.

His reign as heavyweight champ was fairly brief, lasting less than four years, but what Marciano lacked in quantity, he delivered in quality. Seven world title bouts, seven victories, six by knockout. Savor the career record of 49-0. In this age of avarice and mega-million-dollar purses, it may never in the boxing world happen again.

ARCHIE MOORE

© Ted Streshinsky

Light heavyweight 199-26-8 (145 KO)

In the sport of boxing, age often blurs. The temptation offered by fat purses keeps fighters in the ring long past their prime. More often than not, the result is predictably grisly. Archie Moore was an exception to the rule of the ring; he won the light heavyweight world championship on December 17, 1955, at the age of thirty-nine, and held the title for more than nine years. When he finally left boxing, Moore was forty-eight or forty-five, depending on the source.

His mother always claimed Archibald Lee Wright was born in 1913, but the fighter claimed it was 1916. Though the birth records do not shed any light, it hardly matters. Moore, at the age of forty-eight or forty-five, was the oldest reigning world champion ever. Bob Fitzsimmons, the British light heavyweight, was a relatively spry forty-two when he finally relinquished his title.

If good things indeed come to those who wait, Moore is the classic example. Joey Maxim had taken the light heavyweight championship from Freddie Mills in early 1950, knocking him out in the tenth round of their London bout. Maxim defended successfully against Irish Bob Murphy and an aging Sugar Ray Robinson before Moore met him in St. Louis. The fight went fifteen rounds, but Moore won a tough decision. His conditioning, a religion for Moore, gave him the endurance to outlast Maxim in the late going. Moore was known for doing some two hundred and fifty pushups per day to keep his arms strong, and the regimen carried him well past his prime.

Though nearly every fighter he faced in his later years was younger, Moore had staying power. In two hundred and thirty four bouts, he produced a staggering one hundred and forty-five

Light heavyweight champion Archie Moore makes things right with challenger Yolande Pompey in 1956. After ten rounds, the referee stopped the fight.

The Ageless Wonder

knockouts, by far the record for any professional boxer. Moore would reign for nine years and fifty-five days—the longest dominance ever by a light heavyweight. Only heavyweight Joe Louis (eleven years, two hundred and fifty-two days), featherweight Johnny Kilbane (eleven years, one hundred and three days) and middleweight Tommy Ryan (nine years, two hundred and eighty five days) stayed on top of their weight class longer. Moore's nine title defenses sometimes defied the laws of nature.

In 1958, a Canadian named Yvon Durelle knocked Moore off his feet three different times in the first round of their fight in Montreal. Then, Moore won by an eleventh-round knockout. Small wonder, for he was only forty-two at the time.

One thing Moore couldn't do was alter the rules of physics. As a 175-pounder, he was unbeatable; as a heavyweight, Moore was human. Twice, he stepped up to challenge heavyweight champions and twice he was knocked out. Moore was capable of gaining and shedding weight quickly, and in 1955 he challenged Rocky Marciano for the heavyweight title. Moore scored a knockdown in the second round, but Marciano recovered—with the aid of a benevolent referee, according to Moore. Marciano eventually won with a ninth-round knockout. On June 5, 1956, Moore stopped Yolande Pompey as a light heavyweight in ten rounds in London. Five months later, he was in the ring with Floyd Patterson for a shot at the vacant world heavyweight title. Moore finished the fight on the canvas after five rounds, but he was a fighter of forty-three. Patterson was only twenty-one at the time.

Moore's last defense came against Giulio Rinaldi on June 10, 1961. He won a fifteen-round decision and chose never to fight again. He was stripped of his title in February, 1962. But in 1965, at the age of fifty-two (or forty-nine), Moore was back in the ring for an exhibition.

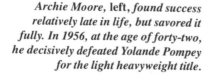

Archie Moore, left, found success relatively late in life, but savored it fully. In 1956, at the age of forty-two, he decisively defeated Yolande Pompey for the light heavyweight title.

Pure Intensity

FLOYD
PATTERSON

PHOTOWORLD/FPG Intl.

Heavyweight 55-8-1 (40 KO)

Floyd Patterson's first heavyweight championship came on November 30, 1956. Rocky Marciano had retired earlier in the year, his perfect career intact, and now the title was vacant. Patterson knocked out the ageless Archie Moore in the fifth round and, at the age of twenty-one, suddenly was on top of the world. Four routine title defenses later (none of which went the distance), Patterson met Sweden's Ingemar Johansson and promptly lost his title when the referee stopped the Yankee Stadium fight in the third round. That was June 26, 1959. At twenty-four, it seems, Patterson was finished. Or was he?

Anyone familiar with Patterson's history should have understood that it was a temporary setback. He was a reticent child and never had the confidence to look people in the face. One of his instructors at a Brooklyn, New York school for emotionally dis-

turbed children thought boxing might unlock the fury inside him. That led, eventually, to the 1952 Olympics, where Patterson knocked out Romania's Vasile Tita in the first round of their middleweight fight in Helsinki. The gold medal won, Patterson embarked on a professional career under the guidance of trainer Cus D'Amato.

For four years, D'Amato brought Patterson along slowly. He was young, after all, and there was no sense in rushing to the top. Finally, in June of 1956, Patterson went twelve rounds for the first time in his life. He survived a durable heavyweight named Tommy "Hurricane" Jackson, despite breaking his right hand in the sixth round. That set up the fight against Moore and the crushing disappointment against Johansson. A rematch with Johansson was scheduled for June 20, 1960, but some observers felt Patter-

Even in a London sparring session, Patterson was a fierce competitor. Dusty Rhodes, left, spent most of his time covering up to avoid the devastating punches of the world champion.

69

Sparring partner Dusty Rhodes, floored by a left hook to the chin, can only crawl away from Floyd Patterson, one of history's most intense champions.

son was overmatched. In fact, a few were already calling Johansson one of history's great heavyweights, though in retrospect they couldn't have been more wrong.

From the time John J. Corbett beat John L. Sullivan for the first heavyweight title in 1892, no heavyweight champion had ever lost the title and managed to regain it. A heavyweight is a delicate machine and, for some reason, resiliency was not in the makeup of the many champions who attempted to win their belts back. Until Patterson. There were times, however, when his intensity threatened to ruin his return.

"I can't rouse myself to work as hard as I should in these sparring sessions," he said one spring afternoon. "The reason I didn't feel up to working hard today is that I got up too early this morning. Couldn't sleep, so I got up at 5 o'clock and did some road work." His trainer, Dan Florio, spent most of his time telling Patterson to relax.

Back at Yankee Stadium, Patterson did not underestimate Johansson. In fact, he finished Johansson with a fifth-round knockout and took back his title. In 1974, Muhammad Ali would become the second heavyweight to match that effort.

On March 13, 1961, the two fighters hooked up for the last time.

It might have been their best fight. Certainly it was their longest. In the first round of the Miami Beach fight, Patterson looked too languid. Johansson floored Patterson twice—with a left hook and then a crunching right to the jaw—for automatic eight counts. The right was the same punch that had taken Patterson out in their earlier fight, but this time he jumped to his feet. A minute later, Patterson had stretched Johansson out on the canvas with a thunderous left hook to the jaw. The Swede scrambled up and the round ended. It was one of the most dynamic rounds in boxing history. The first three minutes, however, left both fighters exhausted. By the sixth round, the boxers were fairly staggering around the ring. Johansson rocked Patterson with a right to the head and for a moment it appeared he would win the fight, but Patterson summoned a three-punch combination that turned the tide. A left hook left Johansson vulnerable for two strong rights to the head.

Patterson was declared the winner and the fight underlined the range of his skill. He was a graceful, fluid fighter who didn't carry himself like a heavyweight. Patterson's hand speed was legendary and his heart, as demonstrated in the Johansson bouts, was that of a champion.

WILLIE PEP

Featherweight 230-11-1 (65 KO)

Gugliemo Papaleo grew up on the poor side of Hartford, Connecticut. He sold newspapers, shined shoes—anything to survive. In 1937, at the age of fifteen, he walked into the Charter Oak Gym and announced, "I want to learn to box. I want to be a fighter."

They told Willie Pep to go home. A few days later, he was back. A scrawny, 120-pounder has to be tough to survive in that atmosphere, and he was. He kept thinking about the advice an older fighter had given him: "When you're in the ring, make believe a cop is chasing you. Don't get caught, don't get hit." The first amateur fight, under his given name, was a success, but the handle wasn't right. They called him Peppie at school, and so a name was born.

Pep won the 1938 Connecticut State Amateur Flyweight Cham-

pionship and took the bantamweight title a year later. Back then, Connecticut amateurs were permitted to accept small payments, and Pep took what he could get. Once, he fought twice on the same card and earned fifty dollars: three times what his father made in a week. His amateur career ended with a 62-3 record. One of those losses was to a fighter named Walker Smith, who outweighed him by twenty-five pounds. Later, Smith would be known as Sugar Ray Robinson.

Pep turned professional in the summer of 1940 and, fighting as if each bout would be his last, won thirty-three in that first year. Pep had won all fifty-three of his professional fights when he was confronted with his first championship opportunity. On November 20, 1942, Pep took the title away from Alberto Wright, the former chauffeur for Mae West and the reigning featherweight

Willie Pep , the featherweight champion, is shown here in a classic boxing stance. It was said that if Pep had chosen a life of crime he would have been the greatest pickpocket since the Artful Dodger.

The Artful Dodger

In 1965, at the age of forty-three, former featherweight champion Willie Pep won an eight-round decision from Hal McKeefer in Miami, Florida.

champ. Though he was legally too young to fight fifteen rounds, he won a unanimous decision from Wright. At the age of twenty, Pep was the youngest man to win the featherweight title since Terry McGovern, back at the turn of the century.

Pep remained undefeated for another eight bouts until Sammy Angott won a controversial decision in March of 1944. That made Pep's record 62-1. Then he was off on another streak, winning twelve bouts in 1943, sixteen more in 1944, only eight in 1945 (because of service to his country), and eighteen in 1946. Heeding the valuable advice from his Hartford days, Pep rarely allowed himself to be hurt. The *New York Journal American*'s Bill Corum dubbed him "Will o' the Wisp." And Red Smith, then of the *Chicago Sun-Times,* was moved to write: "If Willie had chosen a life of crime he could have been the most accomplished pickpocket since the Artful Dodger. He may have been the only man that ever lived who could lift a sucker's poke while wearing eight-ounce gloves." There was the time in 1946 when Pep used his classic head and shoulder feints to win a round from slugger Jack Graves—without throwing a punch!

The year 1947 looked like the end of Pep's boxing career. The plane he was flying in crashed in New Jersey and three passengers died. Pep suffered a broken back and leg, and spent five months in a full body cast. One month later, the man who was told he wouldn't live—let alone box—was back in the ring. He beat Victor Flores in a ten-round decision. "Looking back, I'm still not sure if the accident affected me or not," Pep says. "Some of the oldtimers say it slowed me down a bit, but I was still pretty fast. But I guess breaking your back has to take a little something out of you."

He had won 73 consecutive bouts to run his record to 135-1-1 when he ran into Sandy Saddler on October 29, 1948. The champion was knocked out in the fourth round. Pep won the return match in a fifteen-round thriller. Then, eighteen victories later, Pep met Saddler again and lost the championship in the eighth round after he dislocated his shoulder. Sandler stopped Pep in the ninth round of their fourth fight. He would fight for seven more years, but never with the brilliance that marked his earlier career.

Yet Pep's 230 victories are a professional record that may never be equaled.

Larger than Life

SUGAR RAY
ROBINSON

PHOTOWORLD/FPG Intl.

Welterweight, middleweight 174-19-6 (109 KO)

In boxing's world of harangue and hyperbole, accolades don't usually mean anything unless, of course, they come from a jury of peers. According to some of the century's greatest boxers, Sugar Ray Robinson was, pound-for-pound, the greatest fighter of all time.

"The greatest," Max Schmeling once said. "A distance fighter. A half-distance fighter. An in-fighter. Scientific. He was wonderful to see."

Joe Louis, another admirer, said Robinson was "the greatest fighter ever to step into the ring."

Do not let the 174-19-6 record mislead you. Robinson was very nearly a perfect 142-pound fighter from the outset of his professional career. Born as Walker Smith in Detroit, Michigan in 1921, by the age of seventeen Robinson was the Golden Gloves feather-

weight champion. He would win all of his eighty-five amateur bouts before graduating to the professional welterweight division in 1940.

Robinson was victorious in his first 40 professional fights before he ran into Jake La Motta in 1943. Though he was beaten in a decision, Robinson would fight 91 consecutive bouts without a loss. His record was 123-1-2 over that time—a stretch that may never be equaled for sustained consistency. On December 20, 1946, Robinson outpointed Tommy Bell in New York for the welterweight title. He dispatched a series of contenders, and it soon became apparent that there wasn't a 142-pounder who could touch Robinson.

He was a complete boxer, who, as Schmeling noted, could win in any fashion he chose. Robinson had blinding hand speed, the

On the first leg of his European tour in 1950, Robinson decked Frenchman Jean Stock in Paris.

muscular legs of a sprinter, and powerful shoulders. He danced, he ducked, he deftly slipped punches, and he delivered them with a controlled fury. Above all, Robinson had charisma. He arrived on the scene before Jackie Robinson joined the Brooklyn Dodgers, yet white America didn't seem to notice the color of his skin.

By 1951, Robinson needed a new challenge. Oddly enough, an old opponent—La Motta—would provide the opposition in the 154-pound class. Robinson stepped up without missing a beat; the referee stopped the Chicago fight in the thirteenth round, with Robinson the victor. The Valentine's Day effort demonstrated that Robinson had more than a little heart. He continued on in the middleweight division, with only fatigue and bad judgment ending his muscular string of victories. Nine days after fighting in Italy, Robinson agreed to meet Great Britain's Randolph Turpin in London. On July 10, 1951, Robinson was decisioned in fifteen rounds. Two months later, he won the title back at New York's Polo Grounds in one of history's most memorable fights. Cut over his eye, Robinson fought through his own blood to stop Turpin in the tenth round. After a devastating third-round knockout of Rocky Graziano in Chicago, history beckoned to Robinson again.

Even as he aged, Robinson retained most of his legendary skills. At the age of thirty, he agreed to fight Randolph Turpin in London. Robinson lost this bout, but sixty-four days later he took the middleweight title back by stopping Turpin in the tenth round of their 1951 fight.

"I had won welter and middle, beaten most of the people in my class," Robinson said. "People wanted to see me fight Maxim."

Joey Maxim was the light heavyweight champion and, at 6-foot-1, 175 pounds, was two classes and thirty pounds heavier than Robinson at his natural weight. In June of 1952, seeking to join Henry Armstrong and Bob Fitzsimmons as a titleholder at three different weight classes, he stepped into the ring with Maxim, amidst the 104-degree heat in New York. Through twelve rounds, Robinson was ahead on all cards, but the heat caught up with him in the thirteenth. He never answered the bell for the fourteenth and retired six months later.

Nonetheless, Robinson was in the ring again two years later; his career would run another eleven years. He would twice more hold the middleweight title, but he never equaled the athletic stature of his welterweight days. He transcended boxing's eras—Robinson was a Golden Gloves titlist in 1939, when Joe Louis was the heavyweight champion; when he fought his last fight in 1965 at the age of forty-four, Muhammad Ali was the champ.

Though Sugar Ray Leonard would later appropriate his name, there was only one Sugar Ray Robinson.

MICHAEL SPINKS

Light heavyweight, heavyweight 31-0 (21 KO)

They both won gold medals at the 1976 Olympics in Montreal, but Michael Spinks' mercurial brother Leon was first to make professional boxing headlines when he defeated Muhammad Ali for the heavyweight championship of the world in 1978, at the age of twenty-four. The gap-toothed grin, and bizarre behavior out of the ring, focused all the attention on Leon.

Meanwhile, Michael was carving out a legacy of his own that will stand the test of time. Through 1987, Spinks had fought thirty-one times and won all thirty-one bouts, twenty-one by knockout. On September 21, 1985, he made the successful transition from light heavyweight to heavyweight and decisioned champion Larry Holmes, who was trying to equal Rocky Marciano's record of forty-nine consecutive victories. The critics suggested that Holmes, age thirty-five, lost the fight and downplayed Spinks' role in the victory. So it has always been for Spinks. For most of his life he has been dogged by poor timing, charged with inadequacy.

Spinks was born July 13, 1956 in St. Louis, three years after his brother Leon. They grew up in the Pruitt-Igoe housing project, where living was by no means easy. "Name it," says Michael, "it happened there. I remember this terrible beating I got. I got jumped on by a gang. A big gang of guys, and all of them used to box, too. I'll never forget that. One time, I was getting smacked around the next thing you know, someone's saying, 'Get out of the way, that's my brother.' It was Leon. Somebody was still hitting

It was Michael Spinks, right, who ended Larry Holmes' hopes of equaling Rocky Marciano's pristine record of 49-0 in 1985. Spinks won a decision over the aging Holmes, but critics were sparse in their praise. That's the story of Spinks' life.

UPI/Bettmann NewsPhotos

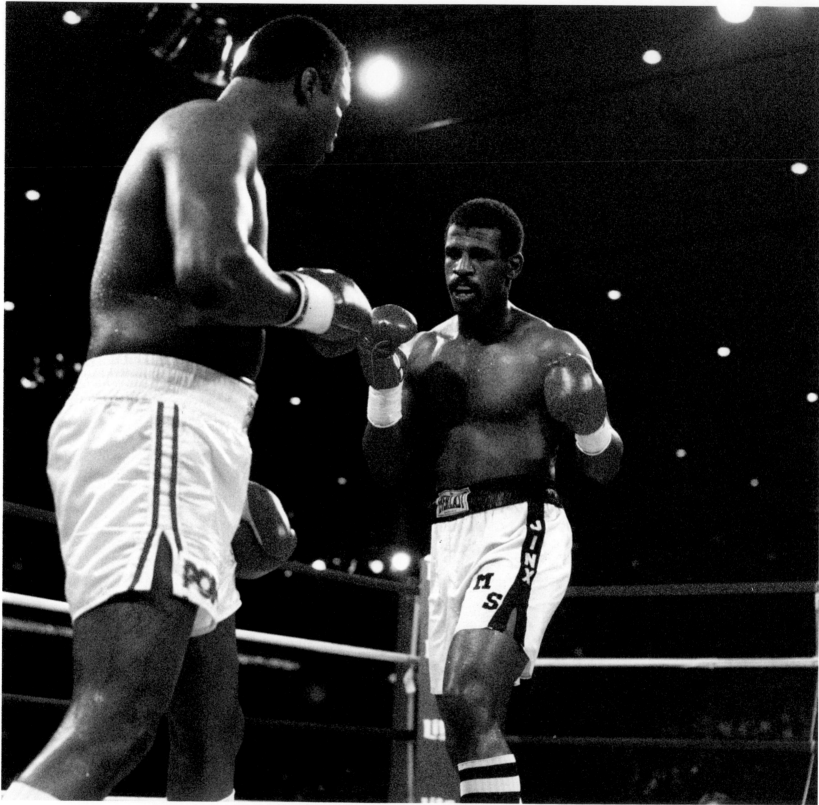

me with a brick while Leon was there. And then someone hit Leon and he said, 'I ain't going nowhere.' And so they backed off.

"Those are some of the fights, the ones that would never leave my memory," Spinks says, laughing. "All those got me prepared for Larry Holmes."

Michael won the Golden Gloves light middleweight title in 1974 and moved up to the middleweight title in 1976. In Montreal, with Sugar Ray Leonard and his brother Leon drawing most of the boxing publicity, Michael very quietly won the Olympic middleweight division. Even the gold medal wasn't enough to satisfy the observers who felt Spinks didn't earn it. Because many of the Eastern-block countries boycotted The Games, Spinks drew a bye in the first round, and won by walkovers in the second and semifinal rounds. A quarterfinal decision over Poland's Ryszard Pasiewicz and a knockout of Russian Rufat Riskiev were his only ring victories.

"There was nobody for me to fight," Spinks says, "but that doesn't mean I didn't earn my medal. I had it out for Riskiev. He beat me in January 1976, beat me pretty bad. He staggered me a couple of times and hit me in my mouth. I couldn't eat solid food for two weeks. But I felt that if I fought him again, I could beat him because I had worn him down in Russia. I had the choice of getting a gold or a silver and I said, 'I'm going for the gold.' I fought like someone who didn't have a conscience."

Spinks held onto that rage as he tore through the professional light heavyweight division. Unlike many Olympic champions, Spinks fought serious contenders to reach the title threshold. On March 28, 1981, he knocked out former two-time champion Mar-

vin Johnson with a left hook that stunned those sitting twenty feet away at ringside. Then, on July 18, 1981, Spinks took the championship belt from Eddie Mustaffa Muhammad in a unanimous fifteen-round decision at Las Vegas. A crushing right to the head in the twelfth round helped Spinks overcome a slow start. In 1983, the World Boxing Association champ unified the title by defeating World Boxing Council counterpart Dwight Muhammad Qawi. Qawi had a reputation for aggressiveness, but Spinks' trademark overhand right in the fight's first minute left the opponent strangely cautious the rest of the way.

By 1985, Spinks had no more mountains to conquer, except the highest. At 6-foot-2, 200 pounds, he challenged Holmes for the heavyweight crown in an attempt to become the first light heavyweight to win the heavyweight title. It was Holmes who had humiliated his brother Leon in a three-round fight four years earlier. Michael had tried to enter the ring that night and stop the fight himself and now he would have the chance for personal revenge. Spinks won, but the fight was less than aesthetically pleasing.

"He wouldn't have lost if I didn't play a part in it," Spinks says. "I made him do all that. He was apprehensive because I was tougher than he was. I stood toe to toe with him from the opening bell. If I ran from him, that probably would have gotten him started. He would have chased me around the ring and waited to drop the bomb. But I intentionally walked to him and stood in front of him. I said, 'If you're going to do it...C'mon with it.' I'm sure he thought I was crazy." But Michael Spinks, one of the smartest boxing champions to ever work in the ring, was crazy enough to win.

Cuban Missile Launcher

TEOFILIO STEVENSON

UPI/Bettmann NewsPhotos

Heavyweight, Olympic Gold Medal 1972, 1976, 1980

In 1956, Laszlo Papp of Hungary did something original. He won the light middleweight gold medal at the 1956 Olympic games in Melbourne with a victory over Jose Torres of the United States. In doing so, Papp became the first man to win three Olympic boxing gold medals. He had previously won the 1948 middleweight crown and the 1952 light middleweight title. In 1980, Teofilio Stevenson of Cuba became the second man to win three gold medals, and he did it in the difficult heavyweight division.

Olympic boxing competition is certifiably the keenest there is. In most cases, a fighter prepares all his life for the event, and the three, three-minute rounds are all he has to prove himself. The pressure is enormous. Over the years, Olympic competition has produced some of the greatest fighters who ever lived. Muham-

mad Ali (nee Cassius Clay), George Foreman, and Joe Frazier all won Olympic gold medals before embarking on professional careers that included world heavyweight championships. Welterweight Sugar Ray Leonard was the Olympic light welterweight champion; three years later he was the world light middleweight champion.

Most fighters from Eastern Bloc countries, like Papp, are never afforded the opportunity to earn prize money in the professional ring. Stevenson is also such an athlete, and one wonders what might have been had he stepped into the ring with Ali, Foreman, Frazier, Leon Spinks, Ken Norton, Larry Holmes, John Tate, and Mike Weaver—all world heavyweight champions during Stevenson's Olympic reign.

Born in Las Tunas, Oriente, Cuba on March 29, 1952, Steven-

Teofilio Stevenson, above, the three-time Olympic champion, may have been the greatest boxer ever—but he never fought professionally. Stevenson, left, slams the United States' Michael Dokes in their 1975 bout at the Pan American Games in Mexico City.

son was only twenty years old when he ripped through the Olympic field in Munich, West Germany. One of his opponents was Duane Bobick, the United States' great hope for the heavyweight gold medal. Bobick had previously beaten Stevenson in the 1971 Pan-American Games, but he was eliminated in the third round of their quarterfinal bout. Stevenson's right hand, which Bobick had earlier exploited, had grown strong and confident with a year of hard training. Stevenson stopped Romania's Ion Alexe in the final and was declared the winner. Immediately, the charismatic 6-foot-3 champion was besieged by offers to turn professional. Some of the offers ran as high as two million dollars. "I don't like professional boxing," Stevenson said. "And I don't like the way professional fighters are handled. I want to be an athlete and that would not be allowed if I turned pro."

Thus, Stevenson turned his attention to amateur competition and won the World Heavyweight Championship in 1974. At Mon-

Here, Stevenson fights Dokes in the Pan American Games in Mexico City. Dokes lasted three rounds with Stevenson, who won the gold medal.

UPI/Bettmann NewsPhotos

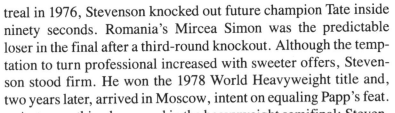

treal in 1976, Stevenson knocked out future champion Tate inside ninety seconds. Romania's Mircea Simon was the predictable loser in the final after a third-round knockout. Although the temptation to turn professional increased with sweeter offers, Stevenson stood firm. He won the 1978 World Heavyweight title and, two years later, arrived in Moscow, intent on equaling Papp's feat.

A strange thing happened in the heavyweight semifinal; Stevenson did not knock his man out. Hungary's Istvan Levai survived all three rounds and though he lost the decision, you would never have known it to see him carry on in the ring. In all nine previous confrontations, Stevenson had knocked his opponent out. Pyotr Zaev of the Soviet Union managed to stay on his feet, but Stevenson was declared the winner. He was one of Cuba's six gold medal winners. The Americans were conspicuously absent, just as Stevenson had chosen to avoid the professional ranks.

Oh, what might have been.

GENE TUNNEY

PHOTOWORLD/FPG Intl.

Heavyweight 65-2-1 (43 KO)

Gene Tunney walked away from the sport that gave him fame, fortune, and a few bloody noses. In 1928, during the Golden Age of Sports that produced Babe Ruth, Jim Thorpe, and Bobby Jones, Tunney was the heavyweight champion of the world. He had earned more than two million dollars, defeated Jack Dempsey in two epic fights that changed boxing history and, at the age of thirty, declared it over.

"I had all the money I needed," Tunney said. "I had not the slightest desire to continue fighting until my ears began to buzz. I wanted to settle down. I think I could have held my peak for another year or two, but I think I made the right decision. Eventually you get licked. Even John L. Sullivan met his master."

So Tunney became his own master and escaped the ring with his features and mind intact. With his fourteen year career as evi-

dence, Tunney has to be rated as one of boxing's greatest heavyweights.

Born on May 25, 1898 above a corner grocery in New York's Greenwich Village, his Irish-American parents christened him James Joseph Tunney. At the age of eight, he was already boxing with the gloves his father gave him. Tunney quit school at fifteen and was boxing regularly, as an amateur, at the age of sixteen. Two years later, he took his first professional fight and knocked out Bobby Dawson in the eighth round. At the time, Tunney weighed all of 140 pounds.

With the arrival of World War I, Tunney joined the Marines. An elbow injury nearly prevented him from enlisting, but Tunney eventually saw combat duty in the Metz sector in France. After the Armistice, the soldiers took up boxing to pass the time. Tun-

Before he became the heavyweight champion in 1926, Tunney was a World War I Marine, in uniform and in the ring.

A Boxer and a Gentleman

Tunney wasn't particularly fierce # looking, but once in the ring he was effective. After missing this left in the 1926 heavyweight bout, Tunney weathered the toughest punch of the fight, a seventh-round right to the ribs from Jack Dempsey. Nonetheless, Tunney took Dempsey's title.

ney knew something about boxing. He won his regiment's light heavyweight championship and soon he was back in the ring professionally. In 1922, Tunney decisioned Battling Levinsky in twelve rounds to become the American light heavyweight champion. Later that year Tunney lost the title to Harry Greb, but outpointed him twice in 1923.

As the years passed, Tunney grew into his 6-foot frame. He soon weighed more than 190 pounds and began fighting in the heavyweight division. On September 23, 1926, Tunney was given a title shot against Dempsey, who had been champion for more than seven years. Most observers gave Tunney little chance of winning.

Dempsey had not defended his title for three years and he looked rusty in their ten-round bout before 120,757 spectators in Philadelphia. Tunney won a decision and the rematch stimulated unprecedented interest. A year later, more than one hundred thousand spectators crammed into Chicago's Soldier Field to watch Tunney survive the famed "Long Count" and decision Dempsey in another ten-rounder. Tunney brought home $990,450 and gave promoter Tex Rickard the $9,555 difference so Rickard could write Tunney a check for an even million dollars.

On July 26, 1928, Tunney stopped New Zealand's Tom "Hard Rock" Heeney in eleven rounds. It was the last fight of his career and was prompted, in part, by his new wife, socialite Polly Lauder. The other factor was Tunney's temperament. Though he had fought for more than half his life, it was never his burning passion. Tunney was offered five hundred thousand dollars to fight Dempsey a third time, but gracefully declined. Tunney would rise to become the director of seventeen corporations, but aside from a few board room struggles, he never fought again.

The Brooklyn Bomber

MIKE TYSON

Heavyweight, 33-0 (29 KO)

He was a child of the 1960s, specifically 1966, when challenging authority was enjoying a new vogue. Mike Tyson never followed the crowd when he was growing up in New York, and by the time he was thirteen years old, reform school was the only place that would or could deal with him. That was where Cus D'Amato found Tyson sparring one day.

"You can be the champion of the world," D'Amato told Tyson. "You've got the size and speed to do it. If you listen to me, and work real hard, I promise it will happen."

Tyson remembers thinking, "What is this crazy 'ol white dude saying to me?"

But this was no idle observer; this was the man who guided Floyd Patterson to the heavyweight title. D'Amato's careful planning made Patterson the youngest heavyweight champion of all time. There were other younger champions—light welterweight Wilfred Benitez, welterweight Pipino Cuevas, and featherweight Tony Canzoneri—but they won titles against relative lightweights. When Patterson took out Archie Moore on Nov. 30, 1956, he was twenty-one years and eleven months old.

As Tyson progressed, it became obvious that D'Amato's eye had not failed him. Tyson was his own man—he wore no socks inside his black boxing shoes and always chose black trunks. Tyson ripped through the boxers D'Amato lined up for him in upstate New York bouts. Of course the opponents were of dubious origin, but D'Amato was trying to teach Tyson the finer points without damaging his confidence, a fighter's best weapon. Both Tyson and D'Amato were throwbacks to a different era. In this

UPI/Bettmann NewsPhotos

Mike Tyson, the youngest heavyweight champion in history, offered a few glaring examples for his success before weighing in for his 1988 fight with former champion Larry Holmes.

modern day, boxers do not fight every month. Yet, Tyson did—
and he won every time, usually by knockout.

By the time he had earned a title shot, Tyson had won each of
his twenty-eight fights, twenty-six of them by knockout. At that
point, his professional career had spanned all of twenty-one
months. On November 22, 1986 with history pressing him, Tyson
required less than two rounds to become the youngest heavyweight champion of all time. He knocked down Trevor Berbick
twice in the second round, and the referee stopped the Las Vegas
fight at two minutes and thirty-five seconds. Then, he would raise
the hand of the champion, aged twenty years, four months, and
twenty-two days.

"I told everybody I expected an early knockout, because I believe in myself," Tyson said. "It's the moment I waited for all my
life."

D'Amato, who became Tyson's legal guardian in 1981, wasn't
there to see his protégé reach the goal he had worked so hard to
gain. D'Amato had passed away a year earlier, but he would have
been proud of Tyson's resolve. Before the fight, Tyson was fined
three thousand dollars for refusing to change his black trunks. The
champion always had the choice of colors, and Berbick had chosen black for psychological reasons. Tyson, in the gruff manner

UPI/Bettmann NewsPhotos

of D'Amato, stayed with what had gotten him there. "I'm sure he was up there watching," Tyson said. "This fight was for him."

Nine months later, Tyson accomplished another rarity. Not since "Neon" Leon Spinks upset Muhammad Ali nearly ten years earlier had the heavyweight title been unified. In the interim, there had been three different championship belts belonging to the World Boxing Council, the World Boxing Association, and the International Boxing Federation. After sixteen months and $22 million, Tyson was the champion of them all. He decisioned previously unbeaten Tony Tucker on August 1, 1987 and, incredibly, complained about his performance.

"I'm a perfectionist," Tyson said. 'As long as I make mistakes, I'm not real happy." Thus, at the age of twenty-one, Tyson was looking for new worlds to conquer. On January 22, 1988, it took Tyson less than twelve minutes to knock out former heavyweight champion Larry Holmes. Tyson's managers predict that he will be worth fifty million dollars in the coming year alone. Critics complained that the 6-foot, 221-pounder was a raw, thickly muscled street fighter without grace or technique. Tyson overpowered opponents with pure power, throwing what he called "hydrogen bombs." And so, the frightening truth persists: Mike Tyson may just be learning how to box.

JERSEY JOE WALCOTT

PHOTOWORLD/FPG Intl.

Heavyweight 50-18-1 (30 KO)

H e was a typical luckless fighter, one of a number of washed-up bums you could find hanging around Camden, New Jersey street corners in the 1940s. Except for one thing: This bum was going to be the world heavyweight champion.

Jersey Joe Walcott had been fighting on and off (mostly off) since 1930, and never really amounted to much. He was born as one of a laborer's twelve children in Camden, on January 31, 1914, and was christened Arnold Raymond Cream. His father told stories about Joe Walcott, the Barbados Demon, who reigned as the welterweight champion in his childhood in Barbados, British West Indies. Arnold Cream decided he liked the name and took it for his own. At least initially, it didn't bring him any luck.

"For a long time I had more work dumping garbage for the Sanitation Department in Camden than I did fighting," Walcott said. "And I was mighty glad to get it."

At the age of sixteen, Walcott took his first fight, and the 135-pounder knocked out Cowboy Wallace in the first round of their September 9, 1930 bout. He received $7.50. Walcott would do anything to make a buck—from washing dishes to pouring cement. After all, he had a wife and six children to support. For a spell, he even accepted $9.50 weekly relief checks. He had retired from boxing when Felix Bocchicchio appeared on Walcott's doorstep one day in 1945. "You've got talent," the wily promoter said. "You can't retire."

Walcott managed a sort of half smile. "I got talent—maybe," he said. "I don't know. But even if I got talent, I haven't got coal. And it's coal that keeps my six kids warm. I'm through."

The weathered face of Jersey Joe Walcott tells the story of his difficult life.

A Noble Survivor

Not quite, as it turned out. Two years later, Walcott found himself at Madison Square Garden fighting Joe Louis for the championship. Louis was the one who discovered Walcott in the first place! During the mid-1930s, Walcott had been one of Louis' sparring partners. While training for his first fight with Max Schmeling, Louis was stunned by a Walcott punch and knocked down. Walcott was handed twenty-five dollars and asked to leave.

It now was December 5, 1947, and Walcott knocked Louis down two different times, only to lose a crackling fifteen-round fight on a decision. This, thought Walcott, was as it should be. The barrel-chested, slope-shouldered fighter who had suffered a life of hard knocks found this just another indignity in a series of unhappy accidents. Walcott sought solace in his Methodist Bible, the only truth and justice he knew. Walcott repaid the relief money with proceeds from the Louis fight and awaited another chance.

His prayers were answered on July 18, 1951. After the loss to Louis, Walcott fought three more times for this title and lost all three—to Louis by a knockout, and twice to Ezzard Charles on

Walcott, left, *lost this 1949 bout to heavyweight champion Ezzard Charles; two years later, at the age of thirty-seven, Walcott won the title back.*

PHOTOWORLD/FPG Intl.

points. Now, Charles was after Louis' record of twenty-five title defenses, and Walcott had proved to be a servicable opponent who drew his share of fan support. What harm could another bout against this fighter of thirty-seven bring? Charles' managers couldn't see the harm in it, so they signed Walcott up for his fifth title fight. In Pittsburgh, Charles' second home, a well-timed left hook delivered Walcott's personal pot of gold. Walcott's seventh-round knockout made him the third-oldest fighter to win a title.

On June 5, 1952, Walcott gave Charles another fight and out-pointed him over fifteen rounds in Philadelphia. It was his last fight as champion. Three months later, Walcott was knocked out in the thirteenth round by a kid named Rocky Marciano. A year later, Walcott fought Marciano again, but this time he was knocked out in the first round. Though Walcott's career was effectively over, sentimental observers chose to remember the good times. When Walcott won the title from Charles, he was given a hero's welcome by 100,000 Camdenites. Walcott rode in a limousine over the very streets he had rid of garbage years earlier.

THE
CONFRONTATIONS

They transcend boxing matches, these great confrontations. Phrases like Dempsey-Tunney, Ali-Frazier, or Louis-Conn bring a standard of excellence immediately to mind. Robinson-Turpin and Leonard-Duran were similar matchups where boxers met two or three times and raised the level of their craft beyond mere sport.

Jack Dempsey and Gene Tunney captivated an entire nation between September 23, 1926 and September 10, 1927, in two epic battles for the world heavyweight championship. More than 225,000 spectators in Philadelphia and Chicago paid more than three million dollars to see these two fighters battle for ten rounds. Tunney won both decisions, the second one on the famed "Long Count," and boxing was never the same.

On July 10, 1951, Great Britain's Randolph Turpin did the unthinkable—he beat Sugar Ray Robinson in a fifteen-round decision for the middleweight title in London. Sixty-four days later the two met in what has been called the "Fight of the Century." Robinson stopped Turpin in the tenth round to regain his title.

Joe Louis' two fights with Billy Conn were classic matchups of power versus speed. Louis won the first bout in 1941 when Conn, the light heavyweight champion, stepped in to challenge him for the heavyweight title. Louis overcame Conn's barrage of early punches and knocked him out in the thirteenth round. Five years and a world war later, Louis knocked Conn out in the eighth round of their anti-climactic rematch.

Muhammad Ali and Joe Frazier, the dominant heavyweights of their time, fought three times in a five-year span, and the world stopped every time they met. In 1971, Frazier won the first bout, earning a fifteen-round decision in New York. Ali won the twelve-round rematch three years later in New York before stopping Frazier for a third time with a fourteenth-round technical knockout in the Philippines' Quezon City.

Sugar Ray Leonard lost the only fight of his professional career to seasoned Roberto Duran in Montreal on June 25, 1980. Exactly five months later, Leonard was an entirely different fighter who taunted and frustrated Duran into his famous 'No mas!' exit in the eighth round of their New Orleans rematch.

All these men possessed great competitive spirit, engaged in battle with uncommon fighters of similar resolve. That made their confrontations greater and more memorable than the considerable sum of their parts.

DEMPSEY
VS.
TUNNEY

O n September 23, 1926, exactly 120,757 spectators paying a total of $1,895,723, stuffed themselves into Philadelphia's Sesquicentennial Stadium for the privilege of watching Gene Tunney fight Jack Dempsey for the heavyweight championship of the world. At the time, it was the biggest event in boxing history. Tunney took Dempsey's crown with a ten-round decision but the rematch that lay ahead would, incredibly, dwarf this spectacle.

Promoter Tex Rickard, who staged the first fight and built the old Madison Square Garden, among other things, was a shrewd man. While public sentiment grew for a second match between the two heavyweight titans, Rickard talked of qualifying bouts for a Tunney opponent. Meanwhile, he searched for a site. New York City, with its $27.50 ceiling on tickets, wouldn't do. A Chicago syndicate offered its new stadium, Soldier Field, a 150,000-seat structure on the shore of Lake Michigan. When Charles Lindbergh crossed the Atlantic Ocean in the *Spirit of St. Louis* during May of 1927, America's attention was temporarily diverted. Dempsey then fought Jack Sharkey on July 21 at Yankee Stadium. In the seventh round, a short left hook dropped Sharkey, and Dempsey had again whetted the public appetite. Tunney left the fight impressed with Dempsey's gameness.

The fight was to take place in Chicago on September 10, 1927.

In the seventh round of their second fight, Jack Dempsey, left, knocked Gene Tunney down but was slow in retreating to the neutral corner. Here, referee Dave Barry reaches the belated count of nine, as Tunney begins to rise and Dempsey moves in.

By August 3, Rickard had already received a million dollars in advance ticket orders. The interest was fueled by rumors that Dempsey had not been himself in the first fight. Blood poisoning in his arm, a three year layoff from the ring, legal and home troubles—all were mentioned as reasons for Dempsey's poor showing. Many couldn't understand the unprecedented interest. "…no future chronicler of our times can fail to note that people will contribute about three million dollars to see two men fight for something less than forty-five minutes," *The New York Times* editorialized. "It will not only be an index of the prosperity of the period, but it will reveal to the historian how much the twentieth-century American was willing to pay for a thrill."

As it turned out, 104,943 spectators paid $2,658,660 for the thrill. Tunney received $990,000 and Dempsey took home $425,000, the greatest sum paid to a non-champion to that time. The crowd never stopped roaring. The first six rounds belonged largely to Tunney, the white-trunked champion, who drew blood from Dempsey and seemed to be wearing him down. In the seventh, Dempsey loosed his best punch of the night, a swinging left hook across a straight left that hit Tunney on the side of the chin. Another left hook along the ropes staggered Tunney. Another right, a left, and a right dropped Tunney to the canvas. "I thought he was finished," Dempsey would say later. "I thought I had become the first guy ever to win back the heavyweight title after blowing it. I hit him with all the punches I had been trying to hit him with in the ring and in my sleep for the past year."

Tunney grabbed the bottom rope with his left hand and shook his head. Later, he would have no memory of the last three punches. Dempsey, meanwhile, went to the nearest corner and placed his arms across the ropes. "Go to a neutral corner, Jack!" screamed referee Dave Barry. "I stay here," Dempsey responded. Disgusted, Barry grabbed him and pushed him across the ring to one of the far corners and then returned to Tunney and began his ten-count—some four seconds after the fact. Tunney, eyes clearing quickly, struggled up at the count of ten and immediately retreated. He back-pedaled from Dempsey as he regained his senses. He ducked nine of Dempsey's wild heaves and launched a straight right hand to the head and another to the chin. Dempsey's legs sagged and the crowd knew he had missed his opportunity. The final three rounds were hopelessly anticlimactic.

Ten deaths across America were attributed to the second Dempsey-Tunney fight, five occurring during the seventh-round knockdown. "The Long Count" had a lasting effect on boxing history, as well. It remains today one of the sport's most controversial moments. "Maybe Gene could have gotten up," Dempsey once said. "Maybe not."

LOUIS VS. CONN

Joe Louis, the heavyweight champion, was tired. It was June, 1941 and he had fought six times in six months. Still, his manager Mike Jacobs couldn't resist making a match with one Billy Conn, a former light heavyweight champion, who grew up in the difficult East Liberty section of Pittsburgh. Conn weighed only 170 pounds, but he had held his own with larger fighters. He was a clever Irishman with deceiving hand speed, but beating the reigning world heavyweight champion seemed out of the question.

Louis, afraid of the perception that he was a bully, came into the fight weighing a ½ pound under 200. The effort to cross that psychological barrier cost him a great deal of strength. Nearly fifty-five thousand people flocked to the Polo Grounds in New York on June 18, 1941 to see what Conn could do with the champion. They got what they paid for. In many ways, it was a classic matchup. Louis had the power, but Conn was just quick enough to stay away from his long reach. Conn deliberately made Louis chase him around the ring, then ducked in and delivered two or three quick punches before retreating. By the seventh round, Louis began to grow visibly tired. "You've got a fight on your hands tonight, Joe," Conn said at one point early on. Louis shrugged, "I know it."

The tenth round revealed Louis' character in a strange way. Conn was backing along the ropes when his right leg slipped out from under him. By all rights, Louis could have taken advantage of Conn's predicament and hit him while he was defenseless. Yet, Louis backed off momentarily. Whether he was demonstrating good sportsmanship or simply supreme confidence wasn't clear. At the end of the eleventh round, Conn returned to his corner and waved his glove triumphantly in the air. In the twelfth, a right-left combination staggered Louis. It seemed to be over; it appeared that Conn would become only the second fighter to defeat Louis, following Max Schmeling's twelfth-round knockout in 1936. With three rounds to go, trainer Jack Blackburn stated the obvious: "You need to knock him out, Joe." Louis nodded and met Conn in the middle of the ring for round thirteen. Now, Conn's corner had advised him to fight cautiously for the duration, but sensing the glory a knockout would bring, Conn did not cover up. Midway in the round, Louis forced an overhand right through Conn's gloves. An uppercut followed, and Conn was suddenly dazed. He lunged toward Louis, in an attempt to clinch the champion. Louis backed away and got off a tremendous overhand right that virtually knocked Conn unconscious. Out on his feet, Conn suffered another left hook and a right before succumbing. His head hit the canvas, grotesquely bouncing up before it finally came to rest. Louis was the dramatic winner.

The fight grossed $451,743 and a rematch was sure to draw more. But World War II intervened and Louis and Conn would have to wait five years and a day before they again entered the ring together. Jacobs had tried to match them in 1942 but the plan had failed. Both fighters were very much in debt when they met again for a June 18, 1946 bout. This time, Louis weighed in at 207 pounds and Conn was a rather stout 182 pounds. Clearly, the war effort and the passing of time had affected their conditioning. Some forty-five thousand spectators turned out at Yankee Stadium to see if the two fighters could recapture their special chemistry. They couldn't. Conn tried to escape Louis for most of seven rounds. Twice, Conn slipped and twice Louis allowed him to rise without swinging, for they had become friends since the first fight. Before the eighth round, Louis told his handlers he was going to step up the pace. A right uppercut and a left hook deposited Conn on his back. The referee declared Louis the winner.

The fight drew a gate of two million dollars, but Jacobs had hoped for three million dollars. It was that kind of rematch. "Everybody seemed to be wondering whether I would still be as good as I used to be," Louis mused in the dressing room. "Seems as if I am, don't it?" Joe Louis would hold the title nearly twelve years, but never would a series stir the general public as his confrontations with Billy Conn.

Billy Conn's Irish eyes never stopped smiling, but it was Joe Louis, **right,** *who always prevailed in their memorable confrontations.*

ROBINSON
VS.
TURPIN

These hyperbolic days, there is a "Fight of the Century" almost every year. Inflation is probably the culprit. But back on September 12, 1951 there was a match that lives up to that glorious billing. That was the night Sugar Ray Robinson fought one of the gamest fights in history to win back the middleweight crown that Great Britain's Randolph Turpin had taken sixty-four days earlier.

Robinson was the best fighter of the era; at 142 pounds he was virtually unbeatable. In the first one hundred and twenty-six fights of his professional career, only Jake La Motta had been able to find a way to beat him. After that loss in 1943, Robinson won ninety-one consecutive bouts. He won the welterweight title in 1946 and, looking for new excitement, moved up successfully to the 154-pound middleweight class. It was La Motta who lost the middleweight belt to Robinson in February, 1951. The new champion toured Europe and fought in Italy nine days before meeting Turpin in London. On his home turf, Turpin outpointed Robinson over fifteen rounds and became the surprise champion. Robinson was devastated.

The rematch at the Polo Grounds in New York was immediately set. Robinson, now 123-2-2, would be given the opportunity to win back his crown in familiar surroundings. A record non-heavyweight title crowd of 61,437 parted with $767,627 to see if Robinson could regain the title. Had he been tired in London, had he underestimated Turpin, or was Turpin simply a better fighter?

Through nine rounds, there was no obvious conclusion to be drawn. The judges themselves couldn't decide: referee Ruby Goldstein had it all even, at 4-4-1, while the ringside judges gave Robinson a slight edge, 5-4 and 5-3-1.

Turpin, however, had managed to rip some of the flesh around the outside of Robinson's left eye. The blood was trickling down Robinson's face, into his mouth; in the tenth round Robinson knew the fight would be stopped soon if he didn't end it himself. For Robinson, the taste of his own blood was a powerful motivator. He immediately hit Turpin flush on the jaw. Staggered, Turpin shuffled but didn't go down. Robinson found another opening, and drilled Turpin with a left to the jaw. The champion collapsed and took a ten-count from Goldstein before getting to his feet and weathering another thirty seconds of well-conceived combinations. With eight seconds left in the round, Goldstein sensed the futility of Turpin's situation and stopped the fight. It was a controversial ending, but Goldstein had good reason. Only a week before, in nearby Madison Square Garden, a fighter named George Flores had died in the ring.

Robinson, clearly, was at the peak of his power in this second fight against Turpin. He would go on to fight for twelve more years, and hold the middleweight title two more times after losing it to Gene Fullmer. Robinson's courageous fights against Turpin largely contributed to boxing experts' considering him one of the greatest boxers of all time.

Although bleeding profusely from his left eye, Sugar Ray Robinson stopped Randolph Turpin in the tenth round of their return bout in 1951 to regain his middleweight crown.

ALI
VS.
FRAZIER

Though Muhammad Ali had first won the world heavyweight title nearly seven years earlier (under the name of Cassius Clay), in 1971, at the age of twenty-nine, he was still at the peak of his physical powers. Yet, following his heart, Ali had lost three of his career's prime years. The United States government succeeded where no other boxer had; Ali was 29-0 when he was denied the right to practice his craft in 1968. His Black Muslim religion didn't permit him to serve in the armed forces, and so Ali lost his title.

In the meantime, "Smokin'" Joe Frazier ran up an undefeated record of his own and claimed the vacated title on March 4, 1968 by stopping Buster Mathis in eleven rounds. Victories over Manuel Ramos, Oscar Bonavena, Dave Zyglewicz, Jerry Quarry, Jimmy Ellis, and Bob Foster added to Frazier's championship claim. When Ali returned to the ring in late 1970, he, too, dispatched Quarry and Bonavena. That led to the obvious fight on March 8, 1971 at Madison Square Garden in New York City.

It was a delicious matchup. Ali was several inches taller, faster

*Muhammad Ali, **right**, was flashier, but Joe Frazier was often steadier. He landed this right in the eighth round of their 1974 fight. Ali won this fight in a twelve-round decision, leading to their much-anticipated third bout.*

of foot and mouth—in short, a true boxer. Frazier was a slugger whose build resembled that of a refrigerator. Frazier's activity in the year before this fight gave him a conditioning edge over Ali, who had looked rusty in his comeback bouts. For fifteen rounds, they traded punches and insults. The punishment they dealt was enormous and could be seen later in their bruised, swollen faces. Then, Frazier's big left hook finally found its mark. Ali later said he saw it coming, but couldn't convince his body to step aside. The punch dropped him to his knees. The judges couldn't help but award the decision to Frazier, and Ali had become mortal with his first professional loss. The plan, according to trainer Angelo Dundee, was for Ali to keep Frazier moving and refuse to trade hooks with a hooker.

It "Must have been a hell of a fight," the former champion sighed after the fight, because I'm sure tired." Ali's jaw and hip joints were so swollen, he was later taken to Manhattan's Flower Hospital. Those people who expected "The Greatest" to fade away after the first defeat were disappointed. The trauma of the past three years had given Ali the quality of resilience. He accepted the verdict and gained an appreciation for Frazier's skill. "All through the fight," Ali said, "I kept thinking, 'My, I just got hit with the left hook again.' Now, I don't get hit with left hooks, you understand, but he was doing it. They was hard and accurate, to the head and to the hips. He just kept coming and coming. If I'd gone down three times and got up and was beat real bad, really whupped, and the other fighter was so superior, then I'd look at myself and say I'm washed up."

But, of course, Ali wasn't. The return match on January 28, 1974, nearly three years later, was anticlimactic. Ali had won thirteen fights and lost one, to Ken Norton. In 1973, Frazier had lost his heavyweight title to George Foreman in Kingston, Jamaica. Though Ali won this twelve-round, non-title fight at Madison Square Garden, no one could have known that a third meeting, some twenty-one months away, would be one of the greatest fights ever contested.

Ali lifted the title from Foreman in October of 1974; then, after a series of undistinguished defenses met Frazier for the third time on October 1, 1975 near Manila. More than four years had passed since they first met, but it was another epic struggle. Frazier was relentless, always stalking the dancing Ali. Ali's jab and ringmanship carried him through thirteen rounds; then he stopped Frazier with a technical knockout in the fourteenth. And when it was over, you couldn't tell the winner from the loser. That was as it should have been, for boxing, with the help of Ali and Frazier, had recaptured the public's attention during a time of volatile change and social unrest.

LEONARD vs. DURAN

It was June 25, 1980, a time when the boxing world was looking for the next Muhammad Ali. Sugar Ray Leonard appeared to be the man. Like Ali, he had won an Olympic gold medal. He, too, had a pretty face and an incredibly glib, articulate manner. All Leonard had to do was beat one of the toughest fighters in the world: Roberto Duran, he of "Los Manos de Piedras," Hands of Stone.

Duran entered the fight in Montreal having already established himself as the world's premier lightweight, at 135 pounds. The Panamanian's record stood at 71-1, with fifty-six knockouts. His only loss came to Esteban DeJesus, a man he twice beat to avenge the defeat. Leonard, the World Boxing Council welterweight champion, had won all twenty-seven of his professional fights, eighteen by knockout. When they entered the ring, Duran's 145.3 pounds seemed to be all muscle. Leonard, at 144.9 pounds, looked extremely young and lean. He had, in fact, just turned twenty-four, giving years and valuable experience away to Duran. In the fight, it showed.

In the final analysis, Duran dictated the style of the fight that he won by unanimous decision over fifteen rounds. An expert brawler, Duran used every nasty trick he knew—clutching, grabbing, holding, clinching, elbowing, shoulders to chin, forearm and head butts. Referee Carlos Padilla seemed content to allow Duran a free hand. Leonard, who was not experienced at going fifteen rounds, was eventually worn down by Duran's attack. There were no knockdowns in the fight, but Duran got off a left hook in the second round that staggered Leonard and kept him back on his heels until the fifth round. Even so, Duran barely won the bout. On three scorecards, a total of only four points separated the two. One example: the Italian judge scored 10 rounds even and gave Duran the fight, 3-2-10.

Leonard, who collected eight million dollars, did not dispute the verdict. "We accept what the judges saw," he said. "We have to take the bitter with the sweet, so there's no bitterness at all. That wasn't real boxing, that was a wrestling match. I won't fight him the same way again. I can move around on Duran more. I want to fight Duran again, I really do...My way."

Duran was unimpressed. "He doesn't want to fight me. But if there's money, I'll fight him any time. And this time, I'll really destroy him—I'll be much better."

Exactly five months later, the two met again at the New Orleans Superdome. As far as Leonard was concerned, it might have been five years. Between fights, Leonard had pushed his weight to 146 pounds, but more importantly had redefined his upper body—and his thinking. "I went to school in the first fight," Leonard said later. Duran, now the WBC champion, also weighed 146 pounds, but looked thick around the middle. Leonard seemed terribly nervous before the fight, but when his namesake, Ray Charles, sang "America the Beautiful," a strange tranquility settled over him. This time, Leonard dictated the pace in memorable fashion.

He opened the first round with constant movement and never stopped. When Duran tried to use his brawling tactics, Leonard was able to effectively counter by holding and hitting. He also had learned how to spin off the ropes. Leonard's hand and foot speed was incredible; he threw combinations so fast, it was difficult to count punches. By the fifth and sixth rounds, Duran began to grow frustrated. Round seven might have been the worst. Leonard started to clown early in the round, mugging and putting his hands down. He made faces and shrugged his shoulders. Leonard would stick his chin out, pull it away, and counter. There was even an Ali Shuffle, a dancing routine of such hubris that Duran snarled in disgust. At one point, Leonard wound up with a sweeping right-hand bolo punch and scored with a straight left jab. The spectators exploded and Duran's eyes watered. For three minutes, Duran had been humiliated. The eighth round was more of the same. With Leonard scoring at will, Duran left the center of the ring at 2:43 and walked toward his corner. "No mas," he said, waving his glove. "No mas." Leonard had earned back his championship belt and became a mature fighter in the process.

"I got cramps in my stomach and whole body and then my arms," Duran explained. "I got weaker and that's why I quit the fight. Yes, I'm ashamed of what happened. Yes, this is it. I'm not fighting any more."

This time, Leonard wasn't impressed. "I beat Roberto Duran, I beat him my way," he said. "The fact that he quit doesn't tarnish my victory, how could it? If I had complained about arthritis, if I had said I couldn't move in Montreal because I had hemorrhoids, who would have believed me? Who's to say he got cramps?

"If you look close at both fights, you'll notice that in the first encounter I was very thin. Duran looked huge. This time around, Duran was thin and I was huge."

Not only did this fight ensure Leonard a place in boxing history, it gave the lightweights a credibility they had never known before. The Leonard-Duran fights spawned a series of big paydays for fighters like Marvin Hagler and Thomas Hearns, and of course, Leonard himself. Even Duran, who would fight many more times despite his early retirement announcement, would benefit from the interest he and Leonard helped generate.

Roberto Duran, the crafty veteran, got the better of Sugar Ray Leonard in their 1980 meeting in Montreal; later, in New Orleans, Duran would walk away from Leonard in total frustration.

THE
GREAT WHITE HOPE

Since Jack Johnson took the world heavyweight title from Tommy Burns on December 26, 1908 in Sydney, Australia, boxing has seen an unending series of fighters filling the role of the Great White Hope. Johnson, born in Galveston, Texas in 1878, was the first black fighter to reign as heavyweight champion. Previously, white men wore the crown—James J. Corbett, Bob Fitzsimmons, James J. Jeffries, Marvin Hart, and Burns. Johnson, a strapping 6-foot-1, 221-pounder, had terrific upper-body strength; his gleaming shaved head made him appear even more menacing.

Johnson's victory over Burns, the Canadian champion, had social and political repercussions. Later, when Johnson stopped Jeffries on July 4, 1910, the win touched off racial rioting when some Southern blacks celebrated Johnson's success. Some even died when they overstepped the bounds drawn by white authorities. Ever since, the ring sentiments of a predominantly white America have been colored by color.

Muhammad Ali has suggested that all the great heavyweight champions, including Johnson, the great Joe Louis and, of course, himself, were black. This simply isn't true; "The Greatest" was also colorblind on occasion. Rocky Marciano, whose career record was an unblemished 49-0, was one of the best ever. Jack Dempsey and Gene Tunney fall into that category, too. But for each of those great white champions there were many boxers whose complexion gave them title aspirations that were based less on talent than hope.

Max Schmeling was a classic case. In the wake of Tunney's retirement, the stout German was awarded the heavyweight title after Jack Sharkey was disqualified from their bout for the vacated crown. Sharkey took the title back two years later, but Schmeling would always carry the banner of Aryan Germany. When he knocked out Louis in 1936, Adolph Hitler and an entire nation saw it as an example of racial superiority. When Louis became heavyweight champion in 1937 by knocking out James J. Braddock, there was no comment from Hitler. When Louis knocked Schmeling out in the

When Max Schmeling knocked out Joe Louis in 1936 for the heavyweight title, Adolph Hitler saw it as an example of racial superiority. When Louis took the crown a year later by knocking out James J. Braddock, Hitler was not available for comment.

first round of their 1938 fight, Nazi Germany was completely silenced, save only for an unfounded claim that the fight was won by a foul.

Even critics of Louis had to admit he was the best fighter in the world. Wrote O.B. Keeler of the *Atlanta Journal:* "Joe Louis now is heavyweight boxing champion of the world, and so far as this correspondent can see there is nothing to be done about it…Our champion fighting man with the fists is Joseph Louis Barrow."

Since the time of Marciano, some Americans have been hoping for a white heavyweight champion. George Chuvalo took Ali fifteen rounds in 1966 but couldn't lift the title from him. Jerry Quarry was knocked out twice trying to achieve the same goal. Great Britain's Joe Bugner fared slightly better, lasting twelve and fifteen rounds in his two opportunities with Ali. Chuck Wepner, the notorious "Bayonne Bleeder," was knocked out in the fifteenth round by Ali, and Larry Holmes dispatched Gerry Cooney (1982), Randall "Tex" Cobb (1982), and Scott Frank (1983) while he was champion.

Sweden's Ingemar Johansson was briefly the heavyweight titleholder from June 1959 to June 1960, between fights with Floyd Patterson. South Africa's Gerrie Coetzee, a white boxer, was world heavyweight champion for just over a year in 1984. He knocked out Michael Dokes in ten rounds, then lost the title when Greg Page knocked him out in eight rounds. And now, even in the twentieth-century, America's search for a white heavyweight champion goes on.

Cooney is a modern-day example of the Great White Hope. At 6-foot-5, 230 pounds, Cooney looks the part of the heavyweight champion. But during his career his heart has never been in the right place, so to speak. After getting knocked out by Holmes in 1982, Cooney fought only three times over a period of five years, boxing for less than seven rounds each time. Yet, Cooney was offered five million dollars to fight heavyweight champion Michael Spinks on June 15, 1987. Spinks destroyed Cooney in 5 rounds. That this bout between Cooney, an inactive former contender, and Spinks, a true light heavyweight, could generate a total purse of twelve million dollars is fairly incredible. Until you remember that Cooney was America's latest Great White Hope.

Gerry Cooney: the most recent fighter to bear the heavy mantle of The Great White Hope.

Was this fight between Jack Johnson, left, and Jim Jeffries the greatest heavyweight bout in history? Many experts think so.

THE
AARON PRYOR
STORY

The previous pages were filled with boxing's success stories. Here is Aaron Pryor's tale of success, excess, and eventual failure in the world of boxing. He is a reminder that all boxing legends are not merely famous. Some are infamous.

There was a time when Aaron Pryor was arguably the best fighter in the world, pound-for-pound. On February 2, 1985, Pryor retained his International Boxing Federation junior welterweight title with a fifteen-round split decision over Gary Hinton in Atlantic City. That made "The Hawk" 36-0 with thirty-two knockouts. But the bottom fell out of his life and he didn't fight again for twenty-eight months.

"I know I let a lot of people down," Pryor says, "so I asked God for forgiveness. God gave me a blessing with my ability to box. I'm not going to waste that opportunity now. I went through some horrible times, but I survived. All my life I wanted to be champion. When I made it, I didn't know how to handle it.

"The wrong people met me and I started doing drugs, and it turned my life upside down. I experienced drugs and what they can do. I want kids to know how bad it is. I tell them, 'Say no to drugs. They'll ruin your life.'"

Pryor knows. He spent much of his twenty-eight months of inactivity in Miami's crack houses. There were charges of rape, kidnapping, and assault on a female guest at his home, and a two-week stretch in the Dade County Jail. The term changed his life.

"I decided to get straight while I was locked up," Pryor says, "and there are no more drugs and no more so-called buddies, the hangers on. I really woke up."

Pryor signed to fight Bobby Joe Young in Sunrise, Florida on August 9, 1987, while he was out on $50,000 bail. Young was an undistinguished 29-5-2 Ohio fighter that Pryor's trainers thought he could handle. The comeback fell apart even before the fight began. "You look a little flabby around the gut," observed Young's trainer, Tommy Parks. Pryor, thirty-one, was furious. He swung wildly at the fifty-nine-year-old trainer with a roundhouse left hand—and missed. Parks landed a right hand of

Aaron Pryor was standing on his own two feet in 1982, after he stopped Alexis Arguello in the fourth round. Five years later, after a dismal effort, Pryor met privately with Arguello, who begged him, "Don't do it again."

his own and bloodied Pryor's mouth. In the seventh round of the fight, after Young had established clear dominance, he knocked Pryor out with a left-right combination. As Pryor, bleeding from the nose, mouth, and right ear, was counted out by referee Bernie Soto, he made the sign of the cross.

"This morning, it hit me in the face," said Pryor the next day. "I hadn't lost a fight since I was an amateur in 1976. Everyone knew I was going to be rusty. What's the big deal? I'm coming back from a dead-end street. You have to start somewhere."

Before the fight, Pryor's handlers were talking about a million-dollar fight with Hector "Macho" Camacho. Afterward, Alexis Arguello, the great three-time champion, spoke to Pryor privately. Arguello, who had lost to Pryor in two previous bouts, begged him to retire. "Don't do it again," he told Pryor.

"I came here to see for myself what he had," Arguello said later. "It's obvious he doesn't have anything, so I told him to give it up. When I fought him, I couldn't touch him with my jab. This kid [Young] landed almost every punch. The drugs have taken too much out of him. I was just being honest with him as a compassionate human being. His reflexes are gone and so is his punching power. If any commission in the world would accept him to fight, it would be terrible. It would be a crime."

Pryor wasn't listening. A day later he talked of future bouts. "I am not a loser," Pryor said. "It's not in my genes. I am ready to kill somebody now."

He might have been talking about himself.

THE
HISTORY OF
BOXING

One can imagine the first boxer—Pithecanthropus erectus duking it out with some gruesome reptile or other amphibious creature. The stance and technique probably weren't textbook perfect, but fear is a marvelous teacher. For thousands of years man somehow did without guns and nuclear warheads: His hands were his primary weapon, a natural means of defense and attack. That makes boxing one of the world's most ancient sports.

Stones from the fifth millennium B.C., excavated near Baghdad, clearly bear portrayals of men engaged in pugilistic tactics. Even then, the hands were protected by wrappings. Nearly every civilization had a version of boxing. The Mortlock Island warriors armed their fists with shark's teeth to increase the stakes. In Greece and Rome, similar versions of one-on-one fighting were hugely popular with the leaders and the public. Until about 400 B.C. fighters would wrap soft strips of leather around their hands and arms. Not only did this protect the limbs, but it increased the power of the blow. Gloves made of hard leather, resembling brass knuckles, replaced thongs. The Romans developed the cestus, a glove weighted with iron and adorned with metal spikes. In Greece, combatants fought to the death. Both the Greeks and Romans believed that spirits of the dead were entertained by boxing matches, and so wouldn't haunt the living if bouts were staged at funerals. Eventually, boxing led to the clash of gladiators. That sport was banned at the beginning of the first century B.C., and boxing lay dormant until seventeenth-century England revived it.

In 1681, Duke Albemarle organized a match at his New Hall home in Essex between his butcher and butler. Not long afterward, boxing came in vogue. James Figg, a man equally talented with a sword or cudgel, opened a school of arms at his London amphitheater in 1719. Figg himself defended a challenge from Ned Sutton to become the first champion of record. He continued to box and taught aspiring fighters at his amphitheater, where many contests took place. As the sport took hold, other amphitheaters opened, one belonging to Jack Broughton at Tottenham Court Road in London.

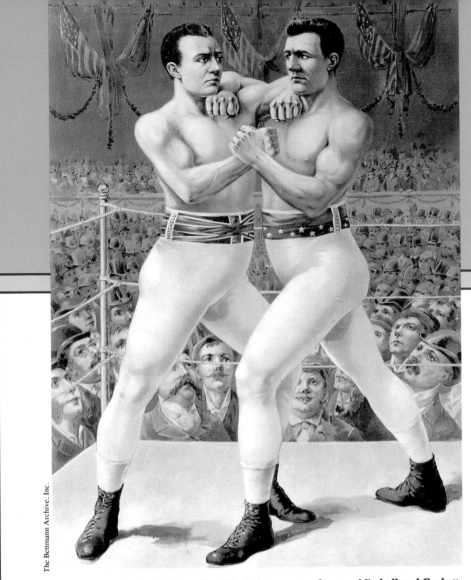

This lithograph shows a bare-fisted fight between two boxers, Mitchell and Corbett. In 1867, new rules were drawn up by the Marquess of Queensberry: there was to be no fighting without gloves.

Today, Broughton is considered to be the father of modern boxing. He fought regularly, and when George Stevenson died as a result of injuries by his hand, Broughton was prompted to create the first set of boxing rules. By now, America had discovered the sport of boxing. In 1816 Tom Beasley and Jacob Hyer met in the first American championship fight. Forty-six years later, America's John C. Heenan and Great Britain's Tom Sayers squared off in the first international bout of significance. In 1867, the Queensberry Rules were drawn up and boxing had become a permanent part of the sporting landscape.

The first world title bout under those new rules came on July 30, 1884, between Ireland's Jack Dempsey and George Fulljames of the United States. In 1891, Canada's George Dixon became the first man to win two world titles, bantamweight and featherweight. In 1903, Bob Fitzsimmons completed a trilogy of titles—middleweight, light heavyweight, and heavyweight—becoming the first man to achieve that feat. Four years later, Eugene Corri of Great Britain became the first man to referee a bout inside the ring. Eventually, the advent of radio and television helped make the sport enormously popular. Now, million-dollar gates are routine. Pithecanthropus erectus would never have believed it.

THE MARQUISE OF QUEENSBERRY RULES

There was a time in boxing when hitting below the belt was a perfectly acceptable means of defeating an opponent. In fact, during the early days of London prizefighting, virtually everything was permitted—including biting, gouging, wrestling, and kicking. Punching, albeit bare-knuckled, was one of the least effective tactics. Contests consisted of a single round that lasted until a fighter was knocked down.

Great Britain's Jack Broughton drew up the first set of boxing rules in 1743. They were basic, including "No second is to be allowed to ask his man's adversary any questions, or advise him to give out." In 1839, London Prize Rules were adopted by humanitarians who were no doubt sickened by the all-too-common sight of blood. These guidelines stipulated that bouts would take place inside a 24-foot square ring, rounds would end when a fighter was dropped, and the two fighters would return after a thirty second respite. Biting, kicking, butting, grappling, and low blows were deemed illegal.

These rules were considered the law of the ring until John Graham Chambers, a former lightweight champion of England, created the Queensberry Rules under the sponsorship of John Sholto Douglas, the Eighth Marquess of Queensberry, in 1867. Douglas, a former amateur lightweight champion, was actually a fine horseman who later gained fame as a steeplechase jockey. His fighting experience at Cambridge University gave him a first-hand knowledge of boxing's flaws, and its unsporting nature. Douglas, who admired the dignity of cricket, wanted to raise boxing's standards, just as London's Jockey Club had improved horse racing.

Shortly after the Civil War in the United States, Douglas and Chambers sailed to America. There, they examined the approach to boxing on the other side of the Atlantic. Upon return, Chambers authored the twelve rules that would forever change boxing.

Gloves were now mandatory, and rounds would consist of three minutes each, with a minute between them. Because the rules were sponsored by Douglas, nobility embraced them as long overdue. John L. Sullivan and Jake Kilrain met in the last world heavyweight title fight contested with bare knuckles. By the mid-1890s, most fighters wore gloves and the Queensberry Rules gained wide acceptance.

It is an etiquette that remains basically unchanged more than 120 years later.

THE ORIGINAL QUEENSBERRY RULES

Rule 1. To be a fair stand-up boxing match in a twenty-four-foot ring or as near that size as practicable.

Rule 2. No wrestling or hugging allowed.

Rule 3. The rounds to be of three minutes duration and one minute time between rounds.

Rule 4. If either man fall through weakness or otherwise, he must get up unassisted, ten seconds to be allowed him to do so, the other man meanwhile to return to his corner; and when the fallen man is on his legs the round to be resumed and continued till the three minutes have expired. If one man fails to come to the scratch in the ten seconds allowed, it shall be in the power of the referee to give his award in favour of the other man.

Rule 5. A man hanging on the ropes in a helpless state, with his toes off the ground, shall be considered down.

Rule 6. No seconds or any other person to be allowed in the ring during the rounds.

Rule 7. Should the contest be stopped by any unavoidable interference, the referee to name the time and place as soon as possible for finishing the contest, so that the match must be won and lost, unless the backers of the men agree to draw the stakes.

Rule 8. The gloves to be fair-sized boxing gloves of the best quality and new.

Rule 9. Should a glove burst, or come off, it must be replaced to the referee's satisfaction.

Rule 10. A man on one knee is considered down, and if struck is entitled to the stakes.

Rule 11. No shoes or boots with springs allowed.

Rule 12. The contest in all other respects to be governed by the revised rules of the London Prize Ring.

CHRONOLOGY

1743 Jack Broughton draws up boxing's first set of formal rules.

1825 Jack Jones defeats Patsy Tunney in Cheshire, England. Jones wins by a knockout in the 276th round.

1855 For the first time, boxers are placed into three different weight classes: lightweight (up to 133 pounds), middleweight (up to 156), and heavyweight (156 and up).

1860 Tom Sayers of Great Britain and the United States' John C. Heenan square off in the world's first title fight. After thirty-seven rounds the contest is mercifully called a draw.

1865 The Marquess of Queensberry authors new boxing rules that become the accepted standard. The most important change specifies three-minute rounds followed by one-minute intermissions.

1868 Tom Dow knocks out Ned Kiely in seven seconds, the shortest bare-knuckle fight on record.

1884 Jim Lawson wins a bare-knuckle bout over Alex Agar in Australia. Agar dies, Lawson is sent to prison for manslaughter, and bare-knuckle fighting is banned in Australia.

1887 Ireland's Jack Dempsey successfully defends his world middleweight title against Johnny Reagan of the United States—in two different rings. A flood interrupts the bout in the eighth round, forcing a move to another ring, some twenty-five miles away. Dempsey knocks out Reagan in the fifteenth round.

1892 James J. Corbett defeats John L. Sullivan in New Orleans to become the first heavyweight champion of the world.

1900 New York's Horton Law, permitting bouts of unlimited duration, is repealed.

1903 Bob Fitzsimmons becomes the first man to win world titles at three different weights. He also becomes the oldest, at age forty.

1904 For the first time, boxing is included as an Olympic sport in the summer games in St. Louis.

1907 During the Tommy Burns-Gunner Moir heavyweight title fight in London, Eugene Corri of England becomes the first referee to officiate inside the ring.

1912 In their world lightweight title bout, both Ad Wolgast and Joe Rivers are knocked out simultaneously in the thirteenth round. Wolgast is the winner when the referee helps him to his feet and counts Rivers out.

1914 Al McCoy, a middleweight from the United States, is the first left-handed world champion. He knocks out George Chip in forty-five seconds, the shortest title fight in history.

1918 Abe "The Newsboy" Hollandersky of the United States retires after his 1,309th fight, an all-time record.

1921 Heavyweights Jack Dempsey of America and France's Georges Carpentier produce boxing's first one million dollar gate in Jersey City, New Jersey.

A match between Johnny Ray and Johnny Dundee is broadcast by Pittsburgh's KDKA, the first boxing contest ever covered on radio.

1922 The inaugural issue of Nat Fleischer's *Ring Magazine*, the "bible of boxing" is published.

Sam Langford of Canada and the United States' Harry Wills meet for the twenty-third and final time in a nine-year span.

1926 More than 120,000 attend the Gene Tunney-Jack Dempsey fight at Philadelphia's Sesquicentennial Stadium, the largest live gate for a title fight in history.

1927 The National Boxing Association, forerunner of the World Boxing Association, is formed.

1931 A live bout is covered for the first time on television by CBS studios of New York.

1934 Italy's Primo Carnera, weighing 270 pounds, becomes the heaviest heavyweight to win a world championship.

1939 Henry Armstrong fights five world welterweight title bouts in a span of twenty two days and is victorious in all of them.

Arnold Sheppard of the United States completes a career notable for 146 losses—a boxing record.

1942 Willie Pep, 53-0, defeats Alberto Wright for the featherweight title at the remarkable age of twenty.

1949 Heavyweight Joe Louis ends his eleven year, 252-day reign as champion—the longest run in boxing history.

1950 Vic Toweel of South Africa knocks down Great Britain's Danny Sullivan fourteen times, a boxing record, before winning in the tenth round.

1951 The Joe Louis-Lee Savold non-title heavyweight fight is the first shown on closed-circuit television.

1953 In the worst year on record, there are twenty-two ring deaths.

1955 Heavyweight champion Rocky Marciano retires with a perfect 49-0 record, joining Jimmy Barry (59-0-11) and Jack McAuliffe (41-0-12) as the world's only undefeated champions.

1956 By winning the light middleweight class, Laszlo Papp of Hungary becomes the first man in history to win three Olympic boxing gold medals.

In his first professional fight, Olympic heavyweight champion Pete Rademacher challenges Floyd Patterson for the world heavyweight title. Rademacher is knocked out in the sixth round.

1958 The third world heavyweight champion to hail from Louisville, Kentucky, is born. Greg Page follows Jimmy Ellis (b.1940) and Muhammed Ali (b.1942).

1960 Lamar Clark of the United States completes a record of forty-four consecutive knockouts.

1963 Sonny Liston and Floyd Patterson each receive $1.4 million for their heavyweight title bout, the first time two fighters shatter the million dollar mark.

Emile Griffith joins Tony Canzoneri as the second man to ever regain world titles at two different weights.

1965 A total of 2,434 spectators attend the Muhammed Ali-Sonny Liston fight in Lewiston, Maine—the smallest crowd for a heavyweight championship bout.

1970 A formidable streak of eighty-eight consecutive victories by Pedro Carrasco of Spain is finally broken when a bout with Joe Tetteh of Ghana results in a draw.

1976 Wilfredo Benitez becomes the youngest world champion of all time by trouncing Tony Petronelli in the third round of their title fight. Benitez is seventeen years, 173 days old.

Michael and Leon Spinks of the United States become the first brothers to win Olympic boxing gold medals.

1977 Eva Shain becomes the first woman judge, in a world heavyweight title fight between Muhammed Ali and Ernie Shavers.

1978 Netrnoi Vorasingh, a light-flyweight from Thailand, becomes the shortest world champion in history. He stands at four feet, eleven inches.

Muhammed Ali regains the world heavyweight title for the third time by defeating Leon Spinks.

1979 Herbert Odom, age forty-six, makes his professional boxing debut against Eddie Partee, age nineteen. Odom wins in two rounds.

1985 Heavyweight Greg Page becomes the title-holder with the shortest reign in history, losing to Larry Holmes seventy-two days after he was proclaimed champion.

Larry Holmes, 48-0, loses for the first time in his career to Michael Spinks in a world heavyweight championship fight.

1986 At age twenty, Mike Tyson becomes the world's youngest heavyweight champion.

1987 Sugar Ray Leonard ends Marvelous Marvin Hagler's nearly eleven year winning streak with a decisive victory in their world middleweight bout.

Thomas Hearns becomes the first man in history to win world boxing titles at four different weights by knocking out middleweight Juan Roldan in the fourth round.

RING CHAMPIONS BY YEARS

HEAVYWEIGHTS

1882–1892	John L. Sullivan (a)
1892–1897	James J. Corbett (b)
1897–1899	Robert Fitzsimmons
1899–1905	James J. Jeffries
1905–1906	Marvin Hart
1906–1908	Tommy Burns
1908–1915	Jack Johnson
1915–1919	Jess Willard
1919–1926	Jack Dempsey
1926–1928	Gene Tunney*
1928–1930	vacant
1930–1932	Max Schmeling
1932–1933	Jack Sharkey
1933–1934	Primo Carnera
1934–1935	Max Baer
1935–1937	James J. Braddock
1937–1949	Joe Louis*
1949–1951	Ezzard Charles
1951–1952	Joe Walcott
1952–1956	Rocky Marciano*
1956–1959	Floyd Patterson
1959–1960	Ingemar Johansson
1960–1962	Floyd Patterson
1962–1964	Sonny Liston
1964–1968	Cassius Clay* (Muhammad Ali) (c)
1970–1973	Joe Frazier
1973–1974	George Foreman
1974–1978	Muhammad Ali
1978–1979	Leon Spinks (d), Muhammad Ali*
1978	Ken Norton (WBC); Larry Holmes (WBC) (e)
1979	John Tate (WBA)
1980	Mike Weaver (WBA)
1983	Michael Dokes (WBA)
1984	Tim Witherspoon (WBC); Pinklon Thomas (WBC); Greg Page (WBA)
1985	Tony Tubbs (WBA); Michael Spinks (IBF)
1986	Trevor Berbick (WBC); Tim Witherspoon (WBA); James "Bonecrusher" Smith (WBA); Mike Tyson (WBC)
1987	Michael Spinks; Mike Tyson
1988	Mike Tyson

(a) London Prize Ring (bare knuckle champion).
(b) First Marquess of Queensberry champion.
(c) Title declared vacant by the World Boxing Association and other groups in 1967 after Clay's refusal to fulfill his military obligation. Joe Frazier was recognized as champion by New York, five other states, Mexico, and South America. Frazier ko'd Jimmy Ellis on February 16, 1970.
(d) After Spinks defeated Ali, the WBC recognized Ken Norton as champion. Norton subsequently lost his title to Larry Holmes.
(e) Holmes was stripped of his WBC title in 1984. He was the International Boxing Federation champion when he lost to Michael Spinks.

LIGHT HEAVYWEIGHTS

1903	Jack Root, George Gardner
1903–1905	Bob Fitzsimmons
1905–1912	Philadelphia Jack O'Brien*
1912–1916	Jack Dillon
1916–1920	Battling Levinsky
1920–1922	George Carpentier
1922–1923	Battling Siki
1923–1925	Mike McTigue
1925–1926	Paul Berlenbach
1926–1927	Jack Delaney*
1927–1929	Tommy Loughran*
1930–1934	Maxey Rosenbloom
1934–1935	Bob Olin
1935–1939	John Henry Lewis*
1939	Melio Bettina
1939–1941	Billy Conn*
1941	Anton Christoforidis (won NBA title)
1941–1948	Gus Lesnevich, Freddie Mills
1948–1950	Freddie Mills
1950–1952	Joey Maxim
1952–1960	Archie Moore
1961–1962	vacant
1962–1963	Harold Johnson
1963–1965	Willie Pastrano
1965–1966	Jose Torres
1966–1968	Dick Tiger
1968–1974	Bob Foster*, John Conteh (WBA)
1975–1977	John Conteh (WBC); Miguel Cuello (WBC); Victor Galindez (WBA)
1978	Mike Rossman (WBA); Mate Parlov (WBC); Marvin Johnson (WBC)
1979	Victor Galindez (WBA); Matthew Saad Muhammad (WBC)
1980	Eddie Mustava Muhammad (WBA)
1981	Michael Spinks (WBA); Dwight Braxton (WBC)
1983	Michael Spinks
1986	Marvin Johnson (WBA); Dennis Andries (WBC)
1987	vacant
1988	vacant

MIDDLEWEIGHTS

1884–1891	Jack "Nonpareil" Dempsey
1891–1897	Bob Fitzsimmons*
1897–1907	Tommy Ryan*
1907–1908	Stanley Ketchel, Billy Papke
1908–1910	Stanley Ketchel
1911–1913	vacant
1913	Frank Klaus, George Chip
1914–1917	Al McCoy
1917–1920	Mike O'Dowd
1920–1923	Johnny Wilson
1923–1926	Harry Greb
1926–1931	Tiger Flowers, Mickey Walker
1931–1932	Gorilla Jones (NBA)
1932–1937	Marcel Thil
1938	Al Hostak (NBA); Solly Krieger (NBA)
1939–1940	Al Hostak (NBA)
1941–1947	Tony Zale
1947–1948	Rocky Graziano
1948	Tony Zale; Marcel Cerdan
1949–1951	Jake LaMotta
1951	Ray Robinson; Randy Turpin; Ray Robinson*
1953–1955	Carl "Bobo" Olson
1955–1957	Ray Robinson
1957	Gene Fullmer; Ray Robinson; Carmen Basilio
1958	Ray Robinson
1959	Gene Fullmer (NBA); Ray Robinson
1960	Gene Fullmer (NBA); Paul Pender
1961	Gene Fullmer (NBA); Terry Downes
1962	Gene Fullmer; Dick Tiger (NBA); Paul Pender*
1963	Dick Tiger
1963–1965	Joey Giardello
1965–1966	Dick Tiger
1966–1967	Emile Griffith
1967	Nino Benvenuti
1967–1968	Emile Griffith
1968–1970	Nino Benvenuti
1970–1977	Carlos Monzon*
1977–1978	Rodrigo Valdez
1978–1979	Hugo Corro
1979–1980	Vito Antuofermo
1980	Alan Minter; Marvin Hagler
1981–1986	Marvin Hagler
1986	Sugar Ray Leonard
1987	John Tate (IBF); Mike McCallum (WBA); Sumbu Kalambay (WBC)
1988	vacant

WELTERWEIGHTS

1892–1894	Mysterious Billy Smith
1894–1896	Tommy Ryan
1896	Kid McCoy*
1900	Rube Ferns; Matty Matthews
1901	Rube Ferns
1901–1904	Joe Walcott
1904–1906	Dixie Kid; Joe Walcott; Honey Mellody
1907–1911	Mike Sullivan
1911–1915	vacant
1915–1919	Ted Lewis
1919–1922	Jack Britton
1922–1926	Mickey Walker
1926	Pete Latzo
1927–1929	Joe Dundee
1929	Jackie Fields
1930	Jack Thompson; Tommy Freeman
1931	Tommy Freeman; Jack Thompson; Lou Brouillard Jackie Fields
1933	Young Corbett; Jimmy McLarnin
1934	Barney Ross; Jimmy McLarnin
1935–1938	Barney Ross
1938–1940	Henry Armstrong
1940–1941	Fritzie Zivic
1941–1946	Fred Cochrane
1946	Marty Servo*; Ray Robinson
1946–1950	Ray Robinson*
1951	Johnny Bratton (NBA)
1951–1954	Kid Gavilan
1954–1955	Johnny Saxton
1955	Tony De Marco; Carmen Basilio
1956	Carmen Basilio; Johnny Saxton; Basilio
1957	Carmen Basilio*
1958–1960	Virgil Akins; Don Jordan
1960	Benny Paret
1961	Emile Griffith; Benny Paret
1962	Emile Griffith
1963	Luis Rodriguez; Emile Griffith
1964–1966	Emile Griffith*
1966–1969	Curtis Cokes
1969–1970	Jose Napoles; Billy Backus
1971–1975	Jose Napoles
1975–1976	John Stracey (WBC); Angel Espada (WBA)
1976–1979	Carlos Palomino (WBC); Jose Cuevas (WBA)
1979	Wilfredo Benitez (WBC); Sugar Ray Leonard (WBC)
1980	Roberto Duran (WBC); Thomas Hearns (WBA); Sugar Ray Leonard (WBC)
1981–1982	Sugar Ray Leonard*
1983	Donald Curry (WBA); Milton McCrory (WBC)
1985	Donald Curry
1986	vacant
1987	Jorge Vaca
1988	Lloyd Honeyghan

LIGHTWEIGHTS

1896 – 1899	Kid Lavigne
1899 – 1902	Frank Erne
1902 – 1908	Joe Gans
1908 – 1910	Battling Nelson
1910 – 1912	Ad Wolgast
1912 – 1914	Willie Ritchie
1914 – 1917	Freddie Welsh
1917 – 1925	Benny Leonard
1925	Jimmy Goodrich; Rocky Knasas
1926 – 1930	Sammy Mandell
1930	Al Singer; Tony Canzoneri
1930 – 1933	Tony Canzoneri
1933 – 1935	Barney Ross*
1935 – 1936	Tony Canzoneri
1936 – 1938	Lou Ambers
1938	Henry Armstrong
1939	Lou Ambers
1940	Lew Jenkins
1941 – 1943	Sammy Angott
1944	Sammy Angott (NBA); J. Zurita (NBA)
1945 – 1951	Ike Williams (NBA: later universal)
1951 – 1952	James Carter
1952	Lauro Salas; James Carter
1953 – 1954	James Carter
1955	James Carter; Bud Smith
1956	Bud Smith; Joe Brown
1956 – 1962	Joe Brown
1962 – 1965	Carlos Ortiz
1965	Ismael Laguna
1965 – 1968	Carlos Ortiz
1968 – 1969	Teo Cruz
1969 – 1970	Mando Ramos
1970	Ismael Laguna; Ken Buchanan (WBA)
1971	Mando Ramos (WBC); Pedro Carrasco (WBC)
1972 – 1979	Roberto Duran* (WBA)
1972	Pedro Carrasco; Mando Ramos; Chango Carmona; Rodolfo Gonzalez (all WBC)
1974 – 1976	Guts Ishimatsu (WBC)
1976 – 1977	Esteban De Jesus (WBC)
1979	Jim Watt (WBC); Ernesto Espana (WBA)
1980	Hilmer Kenty (WBA)
1981	Alexis Arguello (WBC); Sean O'Grady (WBA); Arturo Frias (WBA)
1982 – 1984	Ray Mancini (WBA)
1983	Edwin Rosario (WBC)
1984	Livingstone Bramble (WBA); Jose Luis Ramirez (WBC)
1985	Hector (Macho) Camacho (WBC)
1986	vacant
1987	vacant
1988	vacant

FEATHERWEIGHTS

1892 – 1900	George Dixon (disputed)
1900 – 1901	Terry McGovern; Young Corbett*
1901 – 1912	Abe Attell
1912 – 1923	Johnny Kilbane
1923	Eugene Criqui; Johnny Dundee
1923 – 1925	Johnny Dundee*
1925 – 1927	Kid Kaplan*
1927 – 1928	Benny Bass; Tony Canzoneri
1928 – 1929	Andre Routis
1929 – 1932	Battling Battalino*
1932 – 1934	Tommy Paul (NBA)
1933 – 1936	Freddie Miller
1936 – 1937	Petey Sarron
1937 – 1938	Henry Armstrong*
1938 – 1940	Joey Archibald
1942 – 1948	Willie Pep
1948 – 1949	Sandy Saddler
1949 – 1950	Willie Pep
1950 – 1957	Sandy Saddler*
1957 – 1959	Hogan (Kid) Bassey
1959 – 1963	Davey Moore
1963 – 1964	Sugar Ramos
1964 – 1967	Vicente Saldivar*
1968 – 1971	Paul Rojas (WBA); Sho Saijo (WBA)
1971	Antonio Gomez (WBA); Kuniaki Shibada (WBC)
1972	Ernesto Marcel* (WBA); Clemente Sanchez* (WBC); Jose Legra (WBC)
1973	Eder Jofre (WBC)
1974	Ruben Olivares (WBC); Alexis Arguello (WBA); Bobby Chacon (WBC)
1975	Ruben Olivares (WBC); David Kotey (WBC)
1976	Danny Lopez (WBC)
1977	Rafael Ortega (WBA)
1978	Cecilio Lastra (WBA); Eusebio Pedrosa (WBA); Salvador Sanchez (WBC)
1980	Salvador Sanchez (WBC)
1982	Juan LaPorte (WBC)
1984	Wilfredo Gomez (WBC); Azumah Nelson (WBC)
1985	Barry McGuigan (WBA)
1986	Steve Cruz (WBA)
1987	**Antonio Esparragoza**
1988	**Antonio Esparragoza**

INDEX

Page numbers in italics refer to captions and illustrations.